Praise for the  -Bradley

"Melanie Choukas-　　　　　　　　...ed her place among the storied ᴍᴇᴍᴏᴇʀs of Audubon Naturalist Society who, throughout history, have been our nation's environmental leaders, writers and champions including President Theodore Roosevelt, Louis Halle (*Spring in Washington*), Rachel Carson (*Silent Spring)* and William Weaver (*Beautiful Swimmers*)."
Lisa Alexander, Executive Director, Audubon Naturalist Society

"A spirited, loving, empathetic and expert guide...Choukas-Bradley is mature and confident enough to confront the dark spaces of our world..."
Robert K. Musil, President & CEO, the Rachel Carson Council, Author, *Washington in Spring: A Nature Journal for a Changing Capital*

"If nature is a balm for the troubled heart, this book is a balm for a nature lover in troubled times."
Sadie Dingfelder, *The Washington Post*

"Melanie has emerged as one of America's premier guides to taking a deep breath, looking about with open eyes, and listening to the sanity of the breeze in the trees."
Clay Jenkinson, Author of *A Free and Hardy Life: Theodore Roosevelt's Sojourn in the American West*

"Melanie Choukas-Bradley shows us the way to peace and spiritual comfort in turbulent times."
Bruce M. Beehler, Author of *Natural Encounters: Biking, Hiking, and Birding Through the Seasons* and *Birds of Maryland, Delaware & the District of Columbia*

"Nature does not stop to mourn the damage that we cause to ecosystem integrity or our political fallacies; it keeps striving with each new miracle...Melanie's observations remind us that each day is still a miracle. We only have to open our hearts and take notice."
Susan Leopold, PhD, Ethnobotanist, Director of United Plant Savers, author of *Isabella's Peppermint Flowers*, and member of the Patawomeck tribe of Virginia

"Melanie's writings are deeply centered on the joys of being fully present in our wondrous natural world. The relentless and distressing news cycle can feel like an all-out assault on our sense of wellbeing. Melanie offers us a way to find connection, peace and renewed resolve to fight for what is at stake. Her keen observations invite us to more fully embrace the healing and life-giving forces of nature available to us."
Doug Barker, Founding Board Member, Rock Creek Conservancy, and Chair of Green Ribbon Panel for 125th Anniversary of Rock Creek Park

"There's no better guide to nature in Washington, DC than Melanie Choukas-Bradley. She reminds us that time in nature has the power to restore us to sanity and joy."
Stella Tarnay, Co-Founder, Capital Nature

Resilience: Connecting with Nature in a Time of Crisis

Melanie Chonkis –
Bradley

The *Resilience* Series

Resilience: Connecting with Nature in a Time of Crisis

Melanie Choukas-Bradley

With a Foreword by Wendy Paulson

CHANGEMAKERS
BOOKS

Winchester, UK
Washington, USA

JOHN HUNT PUBLISHING

First published by Changemakers Books, 2020
Changemakers Books is an imprint of John Hunt Publishing Ltd., No. 3 East Street,
Alresford, Hampshire SO24 9EE, UK
office@jhpbooks.com
www.johnhuntpublishing.com
www.changemakers-books.com

For distributor details and how to order please visit the 'Ordering' section on our website.

Text copyright: Melanie Choukas-Bradley 2020

ISBN: 978 1 78904 683 0
978 1 78904 684 7 (ebook)
Library of Congress Control Number: 2020937318

A CIP catalogue record for this book is available from the British Library.

Design: Stuart Davies
Cover and photos by Susan Austin Roth

Interior photos by Sadie Dingfelder, Ana Ka'ahanui and Betsy Bass

UK: Printed and bound by CPI Group (UK) Ltd, Croydon, CR0 4YY
Printed in North America by CPI GPS partners

We operate a distinctive and ethical publishing philosophy in
all areas of our business, from our global network of authors to
production and worldwide distribution.

Contents

Dedication
For the Violets of Spring

Foreword by the Publisher

"What can we do to help?"

In a time of crisis — such as the 2020 covid-19 pandemic — we all have a natural impulse to help our neighbors. John Hunt, founder of John Hunt Publishing, asked this question of our company, and then offered a suggestion. He proposed producing a series of short books written by experts offering practical, emotional, and spiritual skills to help people survive in the midst of a crisis.

To reach people when they need it most, John wanted to accomplish this in forty days. Bear in mind, the normal process of bringing a book from concept to market takes at least eighteen months. As publisher of the JHP imprint Changemakers Books, I volunteered to execute this audacious plan. My imprint publishes books about personal and social transformation, and I already knew many authors with exactly the kinds of expertise we needed. That's how the *Resilience* series was born.

I was overwhelmed by my authors' responses. Ten of them immediately said yes and agreed to the impossible deadline. The book you hold in your hands is the result of this intensive, collaborative effort. On behalf of John, myself, the authors and production team, our intention for you is that you take to heart the skills and techniques offered to you in these pages. Master them. Make yourself stronger. Share your newfound resilience with those around you. Together, we can not only survive, but learn how to thrive in tough times. By so doing, we can find our way to a better future.

Tim Ward
Publisher, Changemakers Books
May 1, 2020

Foreword by Wendy Paulson

When the World Trade Towers were struck on 9/11, I was in New York's Central Park birding with a friend. As the horror of the events became clearer, I found myself returning to the park day after day, along with untold numbers of others. Rarely had I experienced so many people in the park – walking slowly, somber, contemplative, greeting one another in a shared kinship of tragedy. I remember being deeply moved by the warmth and care expressed by people yearning for affirmation of life, finding solace in the beauty and peace of the quiet footpaths that wound through ponds and woodlands and open fields.

After one of those outings, only a day or two after the horrific events in lower Manhattan, I returned to our high-rise apartment. I looked out the window and spotted a kestrel, then a couple more, flying by as they hawked green darner dragonflies. That moment is seared in my memory. Those falcons were carrying on an age-old pattern, one they and countless others pursue every September as they migrate southward, following the simultaneous migration of green darner dragonflies. The perception of that simple, annual odyssey warmed and uplifted my spirits in an indescribable way. No matter how dark, how horrific the recent events, the rhythm of nature continued. It spoke of life, of unstoppable vitality and beauty.

I cannot help but think of that time in the midst of this global pandemic. While the character and scale of the circumstances are very different, the need for comfort and solace is the same. Now living in Illinois, I find both in the bugling of sandhill cranes as they return, right on schedule, to northern latitudes to breed, in the emergence of the early spring ephemerals, in the songs of chorus frogs on warmer evenings.

Nearly twenty years ago I was surprised by the pull of New Yorkers to Central Park. In the current crisis, the news of people flocking to parks and preserves in Illinois and around the country and world – even, sadly, as many of those open spaces are being shut daily – seems completely logical. Nature offers balm to wounded hearts, peace to troubled thoughts, light and life that outshine the darkness and gloom of the daily news. At the beginning of April, I received a message from a good friend in China, with photographs of Japanese waxwings, an elegant bird species. She told me what joy they brought her. Another friend, this one local, sent a photo of a crayfish he had found with scores of tiny offspring on its belly. Space-restricted people around the world are sharing their natural discoveries.

Melanie Choukas-Bradley is another nature enthusiast whose messages I've welcomed during this time. She has described the blossoming of trees and spring ephemerals in Washington, DC three weeks early and the return of eastern phoebes to the Rock Creek Park woodlands.

I first met Melanie months before a crisis of another sort – the 2008 financial crisis – hit our country. Melanie was leading a Saturday hike on Sugarloaf Mountain in Maryland for staff at the Department of Treasury where my husband served as secretary. As we hiked and talked, we recognized in each other a kindred gravitation to the natural world. Melanie already had written several books about nature in the DC area – about Sugarloaf Mountain, local wildflowers, the trees of Washington. I had begun leading bird walks locally, in Rock Creek Park, along the C&O Canal, on Theodore Roosevelt Island. Before departing from Sugarloaf, we promised to reune for walks from time to time. And we did.

Melanie taught me so much – about pawpaws in the floodplain, about winter clues to tree identity, about the distinctive silhouettes of upper branching in different species. She revived in me a long-dormant familiarity with scientific names of plants. Melanie approached every wildflower, every shrub, every tree with reverence and wonder. Her love for the

4

world of plants – for every individual one – was palpable. A walk with Melanie was an immersion into timeless lessons of botany, beauty, spellboundness. She understood, deeply, the uplift and grace and joy that nature can bring. While it was my husband, not I, who was at the center of the financial crisis, I felt the reverberations daily. Walks with Melanie, as well as by myself, were the balm that soothed and anchored.

Since leaving Washington for our Illinois home, I've returned only a few times to the Capital city. On each trip I've contacted Melanie beforehand. Even though she has been, predictably, deep into a new book project, her eagerness to take an outing together has been instant. We've met on the Capitol grounds to meander beneath and scrutinize the many species of trees contributed by states over the decades. Twice we've met at Theodore Roosevelt Island. Even though I had led bird walks there for several years and felt quite familiar with the vegetation, Melanie pointed out features that had escaped my eye, but never hers: an ancient sycamore springing from bedrock at the river's edge, a tall Shumard oak, which is uncommon in the DC area, and a massive silver maple.

She would soon be publishing a book about finding solace on TR Island. She's the perfect person now to write about finding solace in nature in a time of crisis.

During the global pandemic, even more acutely than after the 9/11 days and during the financial crisis, I realize how essential nature is to mankind. It invites, inspires, nourishes, instructs, soothes, gladdens, fascinates, delights. My hope is that when we emerge from this troubling time, people around the globe will find themselves more keenly aware of how blessed we are by the gifts of the natural world – prairies, wetlands, forests, mountains, deserts, oceans, and all their remarkable inhabitants – as well as by wild pockets in cities and towns.

Even more, I hope that the recognition of nature's value leads us to contemplate our individual and collective roles in caring for our planet as it has for us. In the fiftieth anniversary year of Earth Day – in a time that feels unsettlingly bleak – committing ourselves to more active earth stewardship seems a logical and fitting and entirely necessary outcome.

This book, another example of Melanie's tireless, boundless commitment to opening eyes to nature's treasury, should help us on that path.

Wendy Paulson is a Nature Educator and Chair of the Bobolink Foundation

Introduction

Needing to clear my head, I went down to the Penobscot River. There they were...two harbor seals, raising sleek round heads for a few long breaths before rolling under the waves...In the months ahead we can look to nature for these respites. The nonhuman world is free of charge; sunlight is a disinfectant, physical distance easily maintained, and no pandemic can suspend it. Nature offers not just escape but reassurance.

The Pandemic Can't Lock Down Nature.
Brandon Keim, Nautilus

There is not a sprig of grass that shoots uninteresting to me.
Thomas Jefferson

During a time of personal or worldly crisis, such as the global pandemic we're experiencing in 2020, it's easy to slip into anxious and panicked frames of mind and to fall into ruminative thought patterns. What if there was an elixir at our fingertips that could ease our anxieties and help us feel fully present and connected to something larger than ourselves?

Thankfully, there is. Connecting with nature is something we can all do, even if the only way is through an open window or even an indoor potted plant. As I sit at my laptop, sheltering in place in my home office, pink petals are sailing past the window from my neighbor's flowering cherry tree. A bumblebee has just buzzed by and I hear the lusty songs of cardinals singing from the trees. Warm spring smells are rising from the awakening earth.

Because many of the outdoor events I am scheduled to lead for organizations in the Washington, DC area will be canceled for the foreseeable future, I am discovering ways to connect with nature close to home.

In recent years, medical research around the world has proven the mental and physical health benefits of spending time in nature. Dr. Yoshifumi Miyazaki at Chiba University near Tokyo, and Dr. Qin Li at Nippon Medical School in Tokyo, began conducting ground-breaking research around the turn of the twenty-first century, inspiring medical colleagues around the world to study how time spent in nature benefits health. The data is impressive and growing. Studies have shown that spending time in nature lowers blood pressure, lowers stress hormone levels, and increases immunity to disease. The proven mental and emotional health benefits include improved mood, increased focus, a decrease in ruminative thinking (recurring negative thought patterns), relaxation, and better sleep. One study showed that hospital patients recovered from surgery and illness more quickly if they could merely see trees outside their windows. The spiritual benefits of nature immersion, although harder to measure, are perhaps the most significant of all.

As the author of *The Joy of Forest Bathing, Finding Solace at Theodore Roosevelt Island* and several other nature books, I have studied and contemplated the many ways that nature can help us lead happier and more fulfilled lives, inspired by beauty and largely free of ruminative thought. I have led walks for those who are physically and mentally challenged and I've encouraged all of my nature and forest bathing walk participants to find a "wild home."

In this book I will share with you what I would share on one of my nature or forest bathing walks. I grew up wandering the hills of rural Vermont and I discovered the joys of solo woods wandering at a very young age. I never outgrew the urge to explore my immediate natural surroundings, and as an adult, I've structured a career around it, a deeply rewarding if not an especially lucrative one. Today, although I live in a populous and notoriously buttoned-down national capital, where politics is the coin of the realm, my whole professional and social life takes place in the woods in and around my city. I have been leading nature walks—teaching people about trees, wildflowers and ecology—for decades, in places such as the US Capitol grounds, the National Arboretum, Rock Creek Park, the C&O Canal, Theodore Roosevelt Island, and Maryland's nearby Sugarloaf Mountain. I have led tree ID adventures on foot, via kayak and bicycle, and at times all three ("treeathlons"). In recent years, I have also led forest bathing walks in places as wild as the Rocky Mountains and as urban as the Smithsonian Castle's Moongate Garden on Independence Avenue. Most of the friends I have made over the years I have met outdoors, under the trees.

In these pages I will give all sorts of practical guidance including: How to establish a "wild home": How to develop nature connection as a mindfulness practice (integrating meditation, yoga and tai chi); How to become a backyard naturalist and weave nature appreciation and study into your home schooling; How to develop new ways of seeing and being in the world.

As I write, national and local parks are closing their gates, and more and more we are having to rely on our immediate surroundings for nature connection, but this does not mean you have no access to the natural world. I will share what I have learned from my nature-loving friends in far-flung places. They are discovering an expanded appreciation for the wonders of nature as their physical horizons have grown closer to home, along with fresh insights and a renewed sense of purpose as stewards of the earth. See Chapter Seven—Notes from the Field—to hear directly from them.

Chapter One

Establish a Wild Home

Virginia Woodland (Photo by Susan Austin Roth)

We walk much, our worlds shrunk to the backyard, the near neighborhood, a favorite woodland or wayside. You and I have become like Emily Dickinson, the self-isolated poet, who discovered and reveled and wrote about her garden and a rich, imaginative landscape she developed from the confines of her home in Amherst, Massachusetts.
Robert K Musil, President & CEO of the Rachel Carson Council and Author of *Washington in Spring*

On every nature and forest bathing walk that I lead in the Washington, DC area and elsewhere, even during non-crisis times, I always give this advice: If you wish to deepen your connection with nature, find and establish a "wild home."

A wild home can be any nearby natural area: your backyard,

neighborhood garden or park, a nearby woodland or a single tree. The proximity of your wild home to your indoor home is key.

Once you seek a wild home, you may be surprised by the way a natural area or an individual tree calls to you. Tune in to your surroundings, discovering what resonates with you. Then adopt, get to know, and cherish your outdoor place. You'll want to spend as much time in your wild home as you can—during the day and night, in all seasons and all kinds of weather.

In this time of limited mobility the importance of a wild home is more compelling than ever. When Anne Frank and her family were confined to a hidden annex in Amsterdam during World War II, Anne sought comfort in the sight of a horse-chestnut tree outside her window. Anne wasn't able to climb or sit under her tree, but its beauty and stalwartness helped her through the difficult days. She died in a concentration camp at the age of 15, and her tree lived into the twenty-first century. When it succumbed to a windstorm, it was survived by saplings planted around the world in honor of the young girl who loved it. I visit one of them here in Washington, DC as often as I can.

I hope you'll still be able to go outside and spend time in your wild home for the duration of our current crisis. I have two nearby places that I consider wild homes: Rock Creek Park, the oldest and one of the largest urban national parks in the US, which has so far remained open during the current crisis, and our backyard. As soon as our community was asked to stay at home, I ordered a hammock and some vegetable seeds. If the national park should close to visitors, my husband, Jim, and I will have a hammock to lie in and contemplate the clouds and watch the birds, and we'll be able to dig in the dirt and grow some of our food. We are very fortunate, and I will never take the gift of my sheltering homes—indoors and out—for granted.

Why do I encourage people to find a wild home, and not just during times of crisis? Because nature connection is all about intimacy. True intimacy springs from familiarity. Traveling to faraway places is enlightening—both for enjoyment and personal growth. But, it is what we tune into day to day in our familiar realms that is the most essential aspect of our experience and consciousness. Our wild homes teach us how to honor the familiar and delight in the new. Every day that I visit Rock Creek Park, or the world outside my backdoor, I see something constant and which I know well, intertwined with something new that I have never observed before or even imagined. The magnolia tree by our back fence is familiar and dear, but I've never noticed the fuzzy buds unfolding to delicate white spring flowers at just this stage in their opening. As the living things in my familiar world grow, so do I, in awareness and joy.

Our relationships with nature closely resemble our human relationships. When I meet someone for the first time, I may note her name and personal appearance, warmth, intelligence and sense of humor. I receive an impression based on limited information. If we become friends, I will get to know this person over time in all of her moods and in relation to our common experiences. The depth of my love and appreciation will grow with the months and years, as my friend becomes an integral part of my life. She will comfort me with the constant and dependable aspects of her personality and surprise me with newly revealed dimensions.

So it is with a beloved place. Once we get to know a small patch of earth through the days and seasons, our understanding of its moods and rhythms grows. We welcome seasonal change and delight in the ways it transforms our wild homes. In the comfort and dependability of deepening familiarity there is always the surprise of the new. A female cardinal, assisted by her mate, builds a nest in our favorite dogwood tree; a summer shower leaves a rainbow in its wake above a beloved grove of trees. These things will delight us if we are awake and open to them, if we are tuned in with all senses. If unwelcome change arrives, due to climate change or any sort of ecological disruption, we will be the first to notice and to spring to our wild home's defense.

The current crisis invites a deeper connection with all that is nearby. If we are unable to travel even as far as our own workplaces, nature invites us to revel in her constant proximity. My friend and fellow writer Sadie Dingfelder, who normally wanders far and wide around her city *and* the globe, exclaims this week: "I have a newfound appreciation for my tiny porch! I live on the tenth floor of an apartment building in DC's most densely populated neighborhood, and I've discovered a patch of urban wilderness I never knew existed right outside of my sliding glass doors. I write every morning looking through them, and I've made the acquaintance of a pair of dark-colored pigeons, both of whom have a few wing feathers that are pure white. When I'm on the occasional grocery run, I sometimes see that they, too, are out and about in the neighborhood." Sadie, and other nature enthusiasts whom I consulted for this book, have more to say in Chapter 7. Look there for words of inspiration from Sadie and other nature lovers as they search for novel ways to connect with nature during the crisis.

Sadie's pigeon friends (Photo by Sadie Dingfelder)

In his book, *Shinrin-Yoku: The Japanese Art of Forest Bathing,* leading nature and health researcher Dr. Yoshifumi Miyazaki devotes several pages to the ways that houseplants and bonsai trees benefit our mental and physical health. "Most of us intuitively understand," he writes, "that ornamental plants, whether outside or inside the home or workplace, do improve our sense of wellbeing and many studies have proved this. One of the experiments...[described in his book] shows how when subjects simply sat and looked at a houseplant, they experienced both physiological and psychological relaxation." [1]

Chapter Two

Nature Immersion as a Mindfulness Practice

Springtime Violets (Photo by Susan Austin Roth)

Nature helps me work on staying in the moment and only looking for rabbits rather than going down rabbit holes.
Anne Sturm, Barnesville, Maryland

Many of us around the world are familiar with the concept of mindfulness and may engage in a mindfulness practice. Meditation, tai chi, yoga, and other mindfulness practices have become popular, and I believe that there is an ongoing global revolution in our consciousness that is rarely credited for the quiet societal transformation that it is bringing about. Nature immersion, too, is a practice, a bit less familiar, perhaps, but with roots reaching deep into collective and individual memory.

As a species, more than 99 percent of our evolution was

lived in full proximity to nature. The urban life is new. Although we have separated ourselves from nature, physically, psychologically, emotionally and even spiritually, we have never left her embrace, as we are reminded during a time when a tiny microbe has rocked our world. Last week my daughter sent me a text message that had been forwarded to her: "Kinda feeling like the Earth just sent us all to our rooms to think about what we've done."

As a child, you were no doubt enchanted by an ant or a worm crossing your path, by the endless discoveries in a puddle, by the delicious feel of mud between your bare toes. Perhaps an adult or an older sibling didn't share your fascination, thought the worm was icky, the puddle would get you inconveniently wet, and your feet might track dirt across the carpet. Or, maybe that adult or sibling just wasn't as passionate as you were about the wonder of the moment. If what you heard reflected back was disapproval, annoyance, or simply disinterest, you probably switched your focus to things that others in your life valued. And worms, puddles and mud probably were not on that list.

In the 1980s, the Japanese Forestry Agency coined the phrase *Shinrin-yoku* or forest bathing. They began encouraging overworked and stressed citizens of Tokyo and other cities to visit the country's forests and *bathe* in the natural wonders surrounding them: to sit and lie under ancient trees, dip their toes in rushing waters, breathe the healthful air near waterfalls, and inhale all the scents of the cedar and hinoki cypress forests. Shinrin-yoku resonated in Japan, where a reverence for nature is woven into all aspects of the culture through Shinto, Buddhist and folk traditions. Today there are over 60 forests dedicated to forest bathing in Japan and they are visited by hundreds of thousands of people each year. A similar practice arose in Korea, known as *Sanlimyok,* and quiet nature reverence has long been practiced in China, where it is called *Senlinyu.* In Norway, Nature appreciation and connection is known as *Friluftsliv,* translated as "open air living", and the German language has a wonderful word for the sublime experience of being alone in the forest: *Waldeinsamkeit*. While some cultures have long had the vocabulary and inclination for silent nature connection, here in North America the practice of spending quiet time in nature has been largely undervalued since European contact and settlement. Many prominent American thinkers over the centuries have urged people to commune more with nature, including Henry David Thoreau, Ralph Waldo Emerson, the 26th American president, Theodore Roosevelt, and Rachel Carson.

The original North Americans, who cherished and honored nature in all their traditions, were sickened by diseases for which they had no immunity, killed, and relocated to reservations. Many of those traditions, kept alive by Native American descendants of displaced peoples, are being newly honored by those of us who are searching for more nurturing and sustaining ways of relating to the Earth. We owe them a debt of gratitude as we share what were originally their lands.

Just as meditation, yoga, tai chi, qigong, and other mindfulness practices migrated to the West from Asia during the twentieth century and slowly but surely became adopted and adapted by western cultures, shinrin-yoku has followed in their wake and it has been taken up by people already familiar with the earlier practices. A Californian named Amos Clifford was intrigued by Japanese forest bathing and he formed an organization called the Association of Nature and Forest Therapy (ANFT) which has trained hundreds of forest bathing (or forest therapy) guides in North America and elsewhere in the world.

A few years ago, one of my nature walk participants handed me an article in Oprah's magazine about Japanese forest bathing and the North Americans who were practicing it. When I read the phrase "forest bathing" standing under the trees in Rock Creek Park, I felt myself relax into a full body smile. I understood, instantly and intuitively, what it meant: full immersion in the beauty and wonder of nature. I hopped on a plane to California at the first opportunity to participate in one of those walks. Soon after I trained to become a certified forest therapy guide and in the fall of 2017 I traveled to Japan with Amos Clifford, his wife Michele Lott, and a small group of guides to experience *shinrin-yoku* with Japanese guides in mountain forests throughout the country.

How to Forest Bathe in a Time of Crisis

During a crisis, it may not be possible to participate in a guided forest bathing walk, except perhaps online, where ANFT is offering virtual walks led by certified forest therapy guides. According to ANFT's Michelle Hickey, "We've posted them to our social media sites and on our website: www. natureandforesttherapy.org." Many other organizations are offering therapeutic and meditative online nature experiences.

In most places you can still forest bathe as a solo practitioner, or with a small group of people, provided you maintain physical distance if other participants come from outside your household.

A forest bathing walk can be divided into three segments.

One: Unplug! Think of the airplane setting on your phone as "forest bathing" mode, or, better yet, leave your phone at home. Let go of the news of the day, your to do list, and any other worldly concerns. Visit your wild home and find an especially inviting, comfortable spot. Then breathe. I start every forest bathing walk, whether leading a group or on my own, intoning these words from the conservationist and nature philosopher John Muir: "Another glorious day, the air as delicious to the lungs as nectar to the tongue."[2] It's amazing how glorious the day becomes, and how delicious the air feels when you declare it so. During our current crisis, the air is a lot more delicious in many places due to diminished traffic on land and in the air.

If you have previously practiced mindfulness, you may have

a pattern and style of deep breathing that you can bring to forest bathing. If not, breathe slowly and deeply, letting your belly expand. Then slowly breathe out. After a few deep breaths, close your eyes if you're in a place where it feels comfortable and safe to do so and really settle into your surroundings, noticing everything non-visual around you: the songs of birds, wind, running water, and perhaps city sounds, too (although many of our cities are much quieter at this writing); the smells of the earth and trees; the way the air feels on your face; your rootedness — whether standing, sitting or lying—to the earth. After several minutes of stationary sensations, open your eyes and when you do, pretend that you're seeing the world—with all its beauty and magic—for the very first time.

Two: Slowly and quietly explore your surroundings. First, spend several minutes slowly walking, standing, or sitting as you *notice what's in motion*. This sounds like such a simple thing, and it is. However, simply noticing what's in motion is a powerful mindfulness exercise. I can't help doing it now, as the evergreen shrub outside my window is playfully dancing in a fickle breeze above my laptop through the open window. When you *notice what's in motion* you realize what an enchanted world we live in. Everything becomes vitally interesting, each movement of bird, insect, plant, and cloud, and also the tree trunks and stones that are not moving, and are eloquent in their stillness.

After looking for *what's in motion*, you are probably feeling tuned into your surroundings. Next, explore your *sense of smell*. If you have an understanding of botany, you may recognize twigs that are delightfully fragrant with a little "scratch and sniff." In my wild home, I love to do this with spicebush and sassafras, which smell deliciously spicy. Of course, I'm always careful not to harm or break the twig! Smell the flowers and the grass, pick up and smell a small handful of earth if you're in a place where you can safely do so. My friend Ellen Gordon, who lives near

Sugarloaf Mountain in Maryland, finds this especially soothing now. She says: "Sometimes in the garden, I put my nose close to the soil, to really inhale its life scent—always there." Smells are powerful memory triggers and they can bring you right back to childhood or to a remembered romantic interlude.

Spend some time *tuning in to the sounds* around you. Nature offers many soothing and inspiring sounds and we can feel ourselves relaxing in their presence even if we can also hear the hum of nearby traffic. I learned a special trick from a forest bathing guide in the Japanese Alps. If you are near audibly flowing water—a stream, waterfall, or even a garden fountain, stand with your back to the water, close your eyes and cup your ears in front of them, palms facing backwards. You will be amazed by the way the sound of the water is magnified and all other sounds disappear.

Touch is essential to our sense of well-being and during our current crisis many of us are touch deprived. Know your local flora well enough to recognize poison ivy, poison oak, stinging nettles and any other no-touch plants. (Stinging nettles can be handled with gloves if you are foraging for wild greens—see Chapter Five.) Then touch the leaves, hug the trees, pick up and hold stones and loose pieces of bark, anything in nature that draws your attention. If you can safely go barefoot, it not only feels good, but studies have shown that it's good for your health. On that same walk in the Japanese Alps, one of our guides led us barefoot through a painfully icy rushing stream and afterwards, he encouraged us to happily stomp in some warmer mud!

One of my favorite forest bathing invitations is: *Imagine you are a child.* Whenever I give this invitation to a group, I instantly revert to my own childhood. I get an extra spring in my step and find myself playfully exploring my surroundings as I did as a child. In your own yard or wherever there's a place that's safe to explore, you can skip stones, create art with natural objects, sing with the birds, stomp in a puddle, climb a tree. I love to just mosey about, exploring my surroundings. As adults we carry a heavy burden of guilt and worry about human impact on the earth. This invitation allows us to let go and recover the sense of belonging in nature that we took for granted as children. A related invitation is *pretend you're invisible and find a hiding place.* It is deliciously adventurous to crouch under a tree or bush, among large rocks or in any sort of hiding place and observe the world from there. When I first gave this invitation on a forest bathing walk at Brookside Gardens in Montgomery County, Maryland, and then participated myself, I became aware of how much time animals spend in hiding. I could sense the presence of hiding sleeping creatures all around me in the surrounding woodlands as I crouched under a weeping tree in semi-seclusion. I also felt the thrill of escaping the notice of human passersby. Animals have all sorts of ways of avoiding detection to stay safe, and the hiding invitation reminds us that we are animals and we do too.

As I near the end of a forest bathing walk, I like to spend time *communing with an individual tree.* Trees hold mystical powers and have been recognized and even worshipped for this in many cultures throughout human history. In Japan you'll often find sacred trees next to Shinto shrines, encircled with a ritual rope and tassels. Recent studies have shown that individual trees communicate with each other through compounds released into the air, alerting their neighbors to threats from pests and pathogens, and through vast underground networks of mycorrhizal fungi. They even share nutrients with one another through these fungal connections. We are just learning about this "wood wide web" and what we still don't know about plant intelligence, consciousness and communication is boundless. We feel drawn to trees intuitively, for their beauty, stature and longevity, and for their mysterious power. Everyone has her own way of communing with trees, or cacti in the desert, and I always encourage forest bathers to commune in any way that feels comfortable. Sit or lie under the tree, talk silently or out loud, and open your heart and listen to the tree. When you spend time in your wild home, or exploring a natural area outside of it, you will probably feel drawn to a certain tree or trees. You may develop strong attachments to particular trees and I like to imagine that the trees reciprocate our sensibilities.

Three: Transition back to daily life. You may find yourself feeling so relaxed and connected to your surroundings that you don't feel eager to return to your daily routine or for what passes for one during a time of crisis. On guided forest bathing walks we serve tea and snacks, read poetry, share experiences and help each other transition back to our day-to-day reality. When you're alone or with one or two others, it's important to honor the experience you've had and contemplate what you will take back to your indoor home from your wild home. Even when forest bathing solo, I recite John Muir at the close as well as the opening of my walk. In Muir's words: "In every walk with nature one receives far more than he seeks."[3] and "I only went out for a walk, and finally concluded to stay out till sundown, for going out, I found, was really going in."[4]

Forest bathing, like other mindfulness exercises, is a practice. The more often you do it, the more readily you'll achieve the rewards of relaxation, relief from stress, full engagement with the wonder of the moment, and joy. In the words of my wise friend, the artist Ellen Gordon Gordon, "Taking breath outside with full joy in the now, without thoughts of past or future, takes practice."

Integrating Other Mindfulness Practices with Forest Bathing

If you are a meditator or a yoga or tai chi practitioner who suddenly can't go to your classes, or finds herself with little space and time alone in a busy household, bringing your practice into nature is a wonderful way to find the silver lining in the crisis situation. If you practice solo, you will not be alone. You'll be in the company of trees, birds, the sun and the moon.

Personally, I miss my yoga classes and my instructors, and yet I'm discovering the joy of practicing in the backyard. How often have I done "sun salutations" in a dark room in front of a mirror, achieved "half-moon" under a ceiling, and struck poses named for dolphins, crows, dogs, cats, cows, cobras, fish and swans without a critter in sight? I'm learning to love saluting the actual rising sun, watching bees and butterflies through my legs in downward facing dog pose, and feeling my rootedness to the vibrant energy of the earth. The smells coming up from the earth and from the bursting buds of the trees are intoxicating.

Yoga is an integral part of many forest bathing walks in Japan. On a guided forest bathing walk devoted to fragrant trees and other plants in Okutama in the fall of 2017, our group climbed a winding trail that ended at a yoga platform in a grove of Hinoki cypress trees. A yoga instructor was quietly waiting for us on the wooden platform, seated in the lotus position with our mats all laid out in front of her. She then led us in a restorative yoga practice as we breathed the cypress-infused air with its proven ability to boost immunity.

My sister and brother-in-law, Ellie and Hill Anderson, practice tai chi outdoors in all kinds of weather in rural Vermont. During the beginning of the current crisis, Ellie told me: "When warm weather comes and the crisis passes, Long Wind [an organic farm in East Thetford, Vermont] will open classes again and we will practice on the river. It is so restorative to embrace all of the elements while harnessing chi, the energy fields that are part of the biosphere." Whenever I visit Ellie and Hill, or they visit me, I join them in their tai chi practice, stationed between them and mirroring their moves as best I can. We have practiced together in blowing snow in a field in Vermont, under the flowering cherry trees in Washington, DC, and in many other places and kinds of weather. Because my experience with tai chi is so sporadic, I can't experience the deep spiritual benefits that Ellie and Hill do, but I'm grateful for those small glimpses!

When it comes to meditation, I resonate with some of the participants on my forest bathing walks who describe themselves as "failed meditators," I have never devoted myself to an indoor meditation practice with any discipline or regularity, so I've barely glimpsed what I'm missing. However, I do know that when I am in nature, silently witnessing the wonder of the moment, I feel fully and serenely present and it is often a transcendent experience.

You might want to establish a meditation spot in your wild home now, if only to find a quiet place outside a busy household. I have a "meditation rock" in Rock Creek that I visit as often as possible, and in the backyard there will soon be a new hammock, with its window to the sky. Find a little hiding place among the shrubs and trees. Even if you haven't spent much quiet time in nature previously, you will discover how natural it feels to do so now.

If you attend regular religious services, inability to worship with your congregation during the current crisis may be one of the greatest challenges you're facing. Consider creating an outdoor place of worship in the backyard and improvising services there. Or set up a special area to experience online services offered by your church, mosque or synagogue. Some religious and spiritual traditions practice outdoors as a regular custom and may be able to continue with a little distancing. One of my favorite childhood memories was going to outdoor services in the "Chapel in the Pines" in Canaan, New Hampshire where my dad taught in a summer school and my mom served as nurse. It's one of the reasons that I've always associated quiet outdoor time with a connection to the divine.

Chapter Three

Become a Backyard Naturalist

The author (Photo by Ana Ka'ahanui)

You don't have to mind social distancing with a violet. You can bend down and get close enough to peer into its flowering face and breathe deeply of its scent.
Stephanie Mason, Senior Naturalist, Audubon Naturalist Society

During the current crisis, with theaters, restaurants, bars and stores closed, and many familiar forms of non-electronic entertainment beyond our grasp, there's no better time to get close to nature and to become a "backyard naturalist." As I write, springtime is arriving in Washington, DC, and throughout the middle latitudes of the northern hemisphere. Woodland flowers are blooming, birds are migrating, chorus frogs are calling and every day brings new delights to the natural world.

What exactly is a naturalist? *The World Book Dictionary* defines it as: "A person who makes a study of animals and plants, especially in their native habitats." I call myself a naturalist although I hold an English Literature degree from the University of Vermont. Many of the naturalists I know majored in English. It's my view that a love of nature and a love of literature often go hand in hand. One of the most famous American naturalists, Theodore Roosevelt, wrote in his *Autobiography:* "There are men who love out-of-doors who yet never open a book; and other men who love books but to whom the great book of nature is a sealed volume, and the lines written therein blurred and illegible. Nevertheless among those men whom I have known the love of books and the love of outdoors, in their highest expressions, have usually gone hand in hand."[5] Theodore Roosevelt believed that "it is an incalculable added pleasure to any one's sum of happiness if he or she grows to know, even slightly and imperfectly, how to read and enjoy the wonder-book of nature."[6]

When you are lost in a book, you become immersed in a world that can seem as real and compelling as your daily reality. Getting lost in nature is similar: full immersion in a captivating world, even if that world is limited to a backyard or a view of trees through an open window. Things are always happening in nature. There is drama. There is beauty. There are storylines. Events flow, one into the other. If you love to read, you will certainly enjoy the "wonder-book of nature." And unlike the plot and characters of a novel, the wonder-book is real!

When you become a backyard naturalist, you also become a phenologist, even if you've never heard the word before. Phenology is the study of nature's timing: when flowers bloom, trees leaf out, and birds return to nest. Everything in nature is intricately tuned to seasonal change, with tremendous interdependence among species. Zebra swallowtail butterflies lay their eggs on pawpaw trees just prior to the emergence of the pawpaw leaves in spring. When the eggs hatch, the caterpillars have tasty young leaves on which to dine.

Three years ago, we had an abnormally warm, late winter

in the Washington area, followed by a deep freeze in March. Flowers that had been coaxed into premature bloom were frozen in bud or in blossom. A walk around the White House or Capitol was a journey through frozen brown magnolias. Nearly half the cherry blossom buds at the Tidal Basin froze, threatening their blossoming for the first time in their 105-year history.

The cherry trees recovered and were lovely despite their lost blooms, but I sensed a rippling anxiety through the city. Many people were experiencing seasonal allergies weeks sooner than usual during the early and abnormal warming. I coined the phrase "phenology anxiety" and wrote an op ed piece for the *Washington Post* titled "Worried about the cherry blossoms? You may have 'phenology anxiety.'"

I hope you won't experience phenology anxiety as a backyard naturalist, but if you do—most likely because of natural occurrences linked to the advance of climate change—the best remedy is nature immersion. It seems counterintuitive to move closer to the source that is causing you emotional distress. Yet nothing says "life goes on" like life itself. As a budding naturalist you will soon learn the dance of acceptance and activism— learning to love what is, while also acting to mitigate threats to its existence.

To become a backyard naturalist, simply go outside and sit, stand, walk slowly, or do all three. Observe. What do you see, hear, smell and feel? Just as you would do during a forest bathing invitation, tune in to the natural world around you. A forest bather might be content to do just that, but a naturalist wants to understand the science behind what he is witnessing; to begin to understand the nature of the habitat and the life forms interacting within it; to get in touch with the season and its cyclical dramas. Bring a journal with you and begin recording your observations in words and pictures. My friend Kate Maynor, who teaches nature journaling workshops, shares some words of inspiration: "Now is the perfect time to try nature journaling and explore the wonders beyond your windows. Head outside with paper, pencil and your curiosity. When you notice something interesting (and when you're curious, everything in nature is interesting) make some simple sketches and take some notes about your observations, questions and even your feelings. Learning, pleasure and peace await, I guarantee!"

Tina Thieme Brown, an artist who explores nature with pencil, pen, and brush, and—in non-crisis times—invites people to her log cabin studio in rural Barnesville, Maryland on the Countryside Artisans' tours, notes: "My art sketchbook journal has been a steady companion when exploring the natural world since the 1980s. It is how I creatively connect with plants and their habitats. When I sit down to draw, I let myself settle into the world of the plant. As I focus on a leaf, flower or fruit, some small detail that might have escaped notice draws me in. I am there, within the world of the plant, looking closely and tracking how it moves in space, in my sketch. When that sketch/plant insight happens, I find joyful escape. If the drawing is good, even better. But real joy and momentary escape (from this madness) happens when I stay in the moment, seeing the plant anew with pencil discovering the form."

Looking around my home office, I acknowledge that I have about 100 field guides on my shelves: guides to trees, shrubs, wildflowers, ferns, mushrooms, mammals, birds, insects, reptiles and amphibians. My botanist/ecologist friend Carole Bergmann said to me years ago: "You can't have too many field guides" and I took her at her word. I own a good pair of binoculars and a collection of hand lenses that I loan out to my nature walk participants. What would I do if I didn't have all these resources at my fingertips, if I was starting my naturalist journey now, in the midst of a crisis? I turned to my friend and colleague, Stephanie Mason, senior naturalist at the Audubon Naturalist Society, to help me answer that question. Here's what Stephanie said:

"I love my old-fashioned, thumb-paging field guides as they force me to try and figure out ID questions on my own. Plus carrying a book means I've untethered myself from technology for at least a few hours. But what if you don't have a field guide or don't want the weight of carrying one? Then there are oodles of phone apps and online resources you can take with you into the field. Many are free or very low cost. Of course, there is the iNaturalist platform which lets you download a photo you've taken and send it out to other iNaturalist participants for ID help. It offers many other features, as well, and the submitted information can be used for community science efforts.

"If it's birds you're seeking to enjoy, and you lack a pair of binoculars, focus on their songs and calls instead of their plumage. You've always got your ears with you. If you *do* have a pair of binoculars—but not a hand lens [which is the tool botanists use to see plant parts up close at 10x magnification]— you can always invert your binocs and hold them close to the object you're observing. Presto—you've got a powerful hand lens that you were carrying with you all along.

"But really," adds Stephanie, "ID isn't the point of getting outside and immersing yourself in nature. It's the experience. It's the sensory connections—the sights, the sounds, the smells, and more—with the cycles of life that go on under our very noses every day. So what if you're taking a walk and you don't have any of the tools of the trade along with you? Just stop now and spend some time looking at the plant or mushroom or insect that's caught your interest. You don't have to mind social distancing with a violet: you can bend down and get close enough to peer into its flowering face and breathe deeply of its scent. You can even name the plants or animals you encounter yourself, based on something you've observed about them. What made you stop and look at them in the first place? Although I now know that one of the common spring wildflowers in my region is called Spring Beauty *(Claytonia virginica)*, I might re-name it 'Spring

Stars.' On a sunny day in April, its five-petalled flowers open up to create a constellation of glowing stars on the landscape still brown with last year's leaves."

When it comes to learning about nature, you can't learn everything all at once, or even in a single lifetime, but, as Stephanie says, it's *experiencing* nature that matters most. The more you learn about the natural world around you, the more you realize you still have to learn! Find a few plants, birds, insects or animals that captivate you and learn all about them and how they interact within their ecosystems. Record your observations in your journal, with a date and what Kate calls the "meta" data—time of day, weather, temperature and place.

Each one of the field guides and nature memoirs I have written began with a green and white or black and white speckled composition book in which I recorded my observations and questions in the field. I then turned to the experts, my field guides, and during recent years, online sources such as iNaturalist and Cornell's "All About Birds" website, for help with identification. If you have adopted a wild home you'll have a chance to observe your new acquaintances through the seasons, and you will quickly discover how soon things change. Whatever seasonal occurrences you're observing and experiencing now, this too shall pass, with new wonders taking their place. Turning again to one of my favorite naturalists, Theodore Roosevelt, he wrote of the dramatically changing seasonal cycles at his beloved Long Island home, Sagamore Hill, in his *Autobiography*:

"We love all the seasons; the snows and bare woods of winter; the rush of growing things and the blossom-spray of spring; the yellow grain, the ripening fruits and tasseled corn, and the deep, leafy shades that are heralded by 'the green dance of summer'; and the sharp fall winds that tear the brilliant banners with which the trees greet the dying year."[7]

Although better known as a birder, who continued birding while living at the White House, Roosevelt also keenly appreciated wildflowers:

"Long Island [location of Roosevelt's beloved home, Sagamore Hill] is not as rich in flowers as the valley of the Hudson. Yet there are many. Early in April there is one hillside near us which glows like a tender flame with the white of the bloodroot. About the same time we find the shy mayflower, the trailing arbutus; and although we rarely pick wild flowers, one member of the household always plucks a little bunch of mayflowers to send to a friend working in Panama, whose soul hungers for the Northern spring. Then there are shadblow [also called shadbush and serviceberry] and delicate anemones, about the time of the cherry blossoms; the brief glory of the apple orchards follows; and then the thronging dogwoods fill the forests with their radiance; and so flowers follow flowers until the springtime splendor closes with the laurel and the evanescent, honey-sweet locust bloom. The late summer flowers follow, the flaunting lilies, and cardinal flowers, and marshmallows, and pale beach rosemary; and the goldenrod and the asters when the afternoons shorten and we again begin to think of fires in the wide fireplaces."[8]

Today many lifelong naturalists are finding that they have more time to observe and appreciate nature during the current crisis, although perhaps within a more restricted sphere. Here's a firsthand account from Anne Sturm, a lifelong birder and founding member of the American Bluebird Society, who lives near Maryland's Sugarloaf Mountain, about an hour from Washington, DC.

"For about 18 years, I have participated in Cornell's Feeder Watch Citizen Science project. I find that I am feeding much more bird seed than normal just to have the pleasure of enjoying the birds and recording what happens. Usually, I spend less than an hour recording the data. Now, I am spending much more time as I am not filling my days with the normal routines of life. The male red winged blackbirds are looking so beautiful that I am agreeing to nest with each one that flashes his beauty my way.

I am also giving myself the gift of watching more of the web cams that are offered through the Cornell Laboratory of Ornithology and Explore.org. The one that I am visiting every morning and every evening is the Audubon Rowe Sanctuary Crane Camera which takes me to the great Sandhill Crane migration stop over on the Platte River in Nebraska. The sheer numbers of birds, exciting calls and beautiful flight, speaks to something wild or primitive in me — or should I say it brings out my basic connection to all of life.

My current experiences are helping me observe much more in nature. I am watching spring unfold — and how grateful I am that for us in Maryland this crisis is during spring. I can't imagine what it would be like to experience this isolation with two feet of snow and no power. Right now, my nest box trails are calling and I am going to hope that this solitary activity (that does require driving about two miles) will be considered "essential" or be forgiven since I am still physically isolating myself."

Anne reports her nest box data to the Maryland Bluebird Society and the North American Bluebird Society. Her efforts, and those of many others, have helped to increase the populations of eastern bluebirds, whose numbers were greatly diminished in the 1970s.

Citizen Science

Ana Ka'ahanui and Stella Tarnay co-founded the nonprofit organization, Capital Nature, to help people in the Washington, DC area connect with nature. They are promoting nature events throughout the DC area and encouraging residents to participate in citizen science projects. What's great about participating in citizen science (also known as community science) projects is that you don't have to be an expert. In fact, 3.5 million people worldwide participate in Citizen Science. "Citizen scientists" are individuals who are not trained scientists, but whose backyard observations and data collecting contribute to a collective body of scientific knowledge. Ana notes: "Being a backyard naturalist is as easy as snapping a photo with your phone or camera. What are you noticing? It may be the orchestra of birdsong, the unfurling of leaves and flower buds, or the bug crawling on your windowsill. Using free apps like iNaturalist, Seek by iNaturalist and eBird, our nature observations can contribute to scientific research. Data collected can provide helpful information about biodiversity, species behavioral patterns and migration trends. Not sure of that beetle on your back patio? There is a global community of scientists and nature lovers online that will see your observations and help to properly identify them." She adds: "Take time to discover the amazing nature near you, observe with a sense of wonder, and share your findings with naturalists around the world." This can be especially helpful and meaningful during a time of crisis and physical distancing.

Stella observes: "This circumscribed universe of home, and window, and perhaps balcony or garden, is teeming with life. Citizen science, especially when employing phone apps like iNaturalist, becomes a magic lens through which we become aware of our previously unnoticed neighbors."

Ana and Stella participate in the "City Nature Challenge" each spring through Capital Nature, in partnership with The Nature Conservancy and other conservation and nature education organizations in Washington, DC, and elsewhere. In 2019 people in 159 cities around the world participated in a friendly global competition to record the most species of plants and animals in their cities. In 2020, due to Covid-19, the competition element was removed from the City Nature Challenge. Backyard naturalists were encouraged to contribute their findings in a spirit of collaboration and camaraderie with their sister cities around the world during the last week in April. Says Ana: "Washington, DC area organizers decided to extend the spirit of the City Nature Challenge to all of the month of April, designating it 'City Nature Month.'"

Chapter Four

Family Time in Nature

Playtime in Nature (Photo by Sadie Dingfelder)

Family Time in Nature with Arborist and Environmental Educator Lacey Brown

My friend Lacey Brown, with whom I planned nature events when she was the Family Program Contractor for the DC non-profit Casey Trees, and later, Executive Director of Friends of the US Botanic Garden, is making the most of the current crisis with her two young daughters. "Having my girls home from school has turned into such an opportunity to live our lives according to no schedule and to say yes to all the things we never seem to have time for," she tells me.

"I have always felt an instant recharge from nature," she says. "I grew up on 60 acres of vineyards and orchards with adjoining power road trails, and spent my childhood into high school years roaming happily with my dog Baxter. I have always wanted to give my children that same connection with nature...The isolation protocol essentially limits our adventuring. The great outdoors is now the only 'safe space'. We bring our journals, collections bags, magnifiers, identification books. We catalogue our findings, observations and thoughts. We take photos to ID further when we return home. People out on the trail tend to be friendly in the best of times, and even more so in these times, albeit from a distance. On our access trail to the Rachel Carson Greenway, we walk in Sherwood Forest's stream and count the frogs, crawdads, water skaters and schools of fish. We collect litter and graph how many pieces of each kind we find. From Theodore Roosevelt Island [in the Potomac River in DC], we can see the Kennedy Center; we chat about plays and musicals we've seen and plan to attend once distancing is over. From Columbia Island we can admire the cherry trees across the Potomac on the National Mall and Tidal Basin."

Lacey adds, "I have felt myself transform overnight into a calmer, more mindful parent. I didn't really recognize how much toll the stressors of daily life, the schedules and obligations and small interpersonal dramas, had taken. I'm already pondering how to prioritize these explorations once we're through the pandemic."

A few days later I heard from Lacey again:

"And then on Monday, the stay at home order [with more stringent restrictions] came down from our governor. I truthfully had been deeply enjoying the enforced slower pace of life, embracing whatever it was my children wanted to do. I'd felt mentally very calm until this point and suddenly our confines became infinitely smaller. I panicked. Since the order did not go into effect until 8:00 pm that evening, I immediately packed my girls into our car and fled to the shore to a safely unpopulated place that we could enjoy by ourselves. Wide open sky and sea, fresh salty air, blindingly bright sunshine and nothing on the horizon. We found water access off the boardwalk in Chesapeake Beach, right onto the rocks, technically not a beach, since the beach had been closed the previous day. There was no building of sandcastles, running in the waves, searching for shells and other treasures. We clambered over the rocks, balanced at the water's edge and let the waves crash over our feet, filled our toy buckets with water and simply dumped them out again. And it was still perfect."

Lacey had been busy looking for ways to help other children connect with nature: "As an arborist and informal environmental educator, I instantly started brainstorming what I could offer remotely," she says. In her post-shelter-at-home message to me she wrote: "After giving myself the day to collect my wellbeing, I started re-envisioning what sort of educational offerings I could share with other children. A friend whose husband is a professional sailor had been called upon to help with the homeschooling of a friend's children in Europe, and he led a knot tying course over video chat. I realized I could offer a tree-themed story time similar to the one I developed for Casey Trees as their Family Programming Contractor at nature centers and the National Arboretum. I plan to mine my own girls' library for tree and nature-themed books; since their mother is an arborist, their collection luckily leans heavily in this direction. I will intersperse tree stories with favorite children songs with lyrics modified to be tree and nature themed. I can teach them tree parts coordinated to their own body parts for the 'tree hokey pokey'; 'Head, Shoulders, Knees and Toes' becomes 'Crown, Branches, Trunk and Roots'. As a follow up activity, kids can go out into their own yards and take photos of tree parts and email them to me for tree ID."

An E-Interview with Stephanie Bozzo

Audubon Naturalist Society Nature Preschool Director

I asked Stephanie Bozzo if she'd be willing to answer some questions to help families connect with nature during the current crisis. Stephanie is the Director of a wonderful nature preschool just outside Washington, DC. She wrote: "I really enjoyed reflecting on your questions as I watched my sons climbing the trees in our yard and zipping around our neighborhood on their bikes. There is nothing better than children having uninterrupted time in nature."

Here is a portion of our e-interview:

How would you advise families to make the most of their time in nature for learning and enjoyment during the crisis?

Truly, the best and most powerful place to connect with our children is in nature. Oftentimes, it is much easier to say "Yes!" to children's ideas and requests outdoors than it is indoors. When children are in nature, everything falls into place. Nature is the great equalizer. If a child needs to run, jump, climb, balance, or twirl – there is plenty of space and endless opportunities to do so. If a child needs the pull to focus intently and sit still and observe their surroundings, nature offers the perfect opportunity. Whatever children need for self-regulation and inner peace can be found in nature. Sharing whatever brings us joy in nature with our families – be it a walk in the woods, climbing a tree, going for a spring blossom hunt, taking a bike ride or doing some backyard birding – is a wonderful way to connect and share experiences together. Children don't need help finding what they want to explore in nature – all they really need is a trusted adult with whom to share these joyous discoveries. Let children lead the way to show us what soothes their souls in nature and chances are, it's exactly what will soothe our adult souls as well.

Do you recommend any particular exercises, games, or daily practices?

Children (and most adults!) operate best when days follow a familiar rhythm. Every family is unique but balancing outdoor/ active times with indoor/focused activities will help children as they adjust to new routines. Visual schedules are very helpful for children, so they can see the flow of the day and understand what's coming and what has passed. Our family feels best when we've gotten into the woods early in the day, so we start our days with long woods walks which include "sit spot" time. We each have a tree in the woods where we sit for anywhere between 3-15 minutes just breathing and taking time to notice and observe what's happening both in the world around us as well as inside of ourselves. We share our observations with one another as we walk home and very often my children will have noticed a spider spinning her web or a bird building a nest – things they never would have noticed while jumping from stump to stump or playing active games in the same space. Other outdoor times of the day are spent playing games like What Time Is It Mr. Fox, Red Light, Green Light, Mother, May I?, tag and hide and seek. Playing games outdoors together, no matter the weather, is something we do every day. The laughter, camaraderie, and teamwork involved always leaves us feeling happier and more connected to one another. We end each day with a "good night" walk in which we wish good night to things we pass and chat about our favorite discoveries or activities of the day.

Name three or more fun things you do with your preschool classes.

Journaling and storytelling – We love to give students journal prompts (both fictional and non-fictional) which offer them an outlet to express their incredible ideas through artwork and dictations. Extending their journal entries into storytelling opportunities with puppets (plush or paper) extends the experience for children, allowing them to be actors and directors of something bigger than themselves. Children's imaginations soar when given the space to create.

Science experiments – Children learn best by DOING! Very simple science experiments like making ooey gooey Oobleck, Gak, Slime, and Play Dough keep children engrossed and engaged. Taking separate ingredients and learning how to combine them into something new is always exciting for children. Baking and cooking projects are also fabulous opportunities to experiment in the kitchen together.

Sensory activities – Every child loves to explore with their senses. Creating opportunities for sensory play is as simple as pouring a bucket of water on a dirt patch outside and giving children spoons or trowels and some empty buckets or recycled materials. No dirt patches to be found? Kids love to fill an empty under-the-bed storage box with different media (think: dry rice, beans, flour, or pasta) and measuring cups and recycled items for pouring, measuring, filling and dumping. In no time at all, imaginative play will inevitably start flowing!

Anything else that will inspire and educate?

One recommendation I have been making is for families to keep a photo journal. This is a unique time in history and it will (hopefully) be a once in a lifetime experience. Our children will tell the stories of this time in their lives for many, many years. Keeping a photo journal of what we did, saw, made, and experienced during this time will shape our children's memories in the years to come. Consciously choosing what we focus on to add into our photo journals sets an intention for ourselves to find the beauty and joy in each day and highlight it for our children and families. I often remind myself, "We see more of whatever we notice" – so let your energy flow to what you want to see more of in the world!

Chapter Five

Hands in the Dirt: Gardening and Foraging for Wild Food During the Crisis

Turnip Harvest (Photo by Susan Austin Roth)

I had my hands in the dirt today. I have a connection to the earth and somehow need to be in there, tossing compost, pulling weeds out of it, and prepping garden beds.
Tina Brown, Barnesville, Maryland

At the advent of the current crisis, I was seized with the desire to plant vegetables. It was St. Patrick's Day and I remembered the saying, "Plant your peas by St. Patty's Day." Suddenly that was all I wanted to do but I had no peas and nowhere to plant them unless I wanted to feed Peter Rabbit.

I was not the only one who had this response. Clay Jenkinson, who lives in Bismarck, North Dakota told me, "Up to now, my garden has been a kind of playground, even a Jeffersonian pose. Now I feel that I may need the fresh produce. So I'm going to be more vigilant in going after weeds this summer, water in a more targeted and careful way, and grow some vegetables that I normally would just buy in stores or the farmers markets. My goal is to freeze 200 quarts of creamed corn in September, and can 40 quarts of cucumber pickles and 100 jars of spaghetti sauce."

Although Clay's vision is far more ambitious than mine, I'm now searching for the spots with the most sunlight in our yard and plotting ways to improvise a rabbit fence. I don't know if I will succeed but in the meantime, I've become a forager, noting and often sampling all the edible plants along my walking routes. This morning, as I visited the backyard for my initial dose of sunlight, I noticed that the lawn was brimming with purple violets (a native species actually called "common blue violet"), whose leaves and flowers are edible. I enjoyed a morning snack of flowers and leaves (which are rich in vitamins A and C) and then tiptoed into the front yard to nibble some flowers from our redbud tree, which are also bursting with vitamin C.

This too is a common experience during the current crisis, according to Ellen Gordon, who lives near Maryland's Sugarloaf Mountain. "While walking the dogs over the neighboring farm's fields, I remembered the stinging nettles that used to frustrate the field's owner—but delighted me. They're still there in multitudes! I went back the next day with a large garden basket and filled it to the brim. Mostly I wore gloves, but there was something familiar and comforting about the couple of light stings I did experience—my fingers tingled for several hours afterwards, a reminder that nothing had changed about nettles! Some gathered that day went to making tea, and some into a frittata (heating them neutralizes the sting), while the remainder got dried and powdered for many future uses. Nettles are amazing packets of nutrition, brimming with minerals and

44

vitamins, and I feel like I've welcomed an old friend back into my life!"

With trips to the grocery store suddenly hazardous to our health and shelves often empty, many of my friends are doubling down as vegetable gardeners and foragers. I suspect, as with me, that the need runs deeper than mere food safety and convenience. It's a hunger for connection with the earth, with the elemental feel of dirt between fingers, with the miracle of growth. Also, with the reassurance that we can feed ourselves.

I have written in my books and said to my nature walk participants many times, in a rather abstract and academic way, imagine how closely connected to nature people were when they knew it intimately as the direct source of their foods and medicines. Perhaps this crisis can serve as an invitation to return to ourselves as growers, not just consumers, and as wild plant knowers and foragers.

Gardening is a very big and often frustrating commitment and foraging is something you don't safely do unless you know your plants and have sustainable methods to harvest them without depleting native species. Nature produces many poisons, poisons which protect plants and animals from predation and disease. Ill-informed foragers can sicken and die. However, if you're thinking of planting a garden or learning which wild plants you can safely and healthfully eat, read on. I've consulted my photographer and gardener buddy, Susan Austin Roth, who lives in the Blue Ridge Mountains near Charlottesville, Virginia and my friend and forager Matt Cohen, owner of Matt's Habitats and the foremost forager in the DC area, to share their knowledge and wisdom. Their experiences and advice may help you along your own green pathway.

During World War II American patriots planted "Victory Gardens." Susan is planting hers in 2020. An experienced gardener, and author of ten gardening books, she has no illusions about how difficult it may be.

Susan Austin Roth's Victory Garden

Susan Austin Roth: Saturday, March 21, 2020, Greene County, Virginia

"It's been three weeks since the first case of Covid-19 was diagnosed in the US. I tell my warm-hearted neighbor Jeanette, as we talk across the gap between our vehicles, which are pulled up alongside each other in the middle of the dirt road, facing opposite directions, engines turned off, that I don't think she can catch the disease from the air as she suspects. At least not from the air on our neighboring farms. Not right now, anyway. She and her husband raise cattle, and my partner Jim and I raise Nature, as I like to say. We have been endeavoring to transform 15 acres of our sterile hayfields into meadows of warm-season grasses and wildflowers, and to save our 110 acres of forest from the throes of invasive plants. I know Jeanette appreciates what we are doing here, unlike some other neighbors who find us completely crazy.

Jeanette and I decide we are going to plant our vegetable gardens right away, because she has heard the grocery shelves are empty. I confirm that I have witnessed firsthand that there was no chicken, hamburger or pork left in the meat coolers at Food Lion, Harris Teeter and Costco for the last two days. She's been too busy birthing young calves to have ventured to the market.

I race to Loews and purchase seedlings of red cabbage and Boston lettuce. I add packets of seeds for snow peas, leaf lettuce and spinach. I buy four packages of spinach. Jim likes spinach. He doesn't like Swiss chard. And spinach is easy to grow if the temperatures stay cool. I buy the type that is slow to bolt when the weather warms.

These cool-season vegetables will be the beginning of my Victory Garden. Like my grandfather during WWII, I will grow armfuls of vegetables to keep us alive and nourished with vitamins and anti-oxidants. I decide to include seeds for green beans, summer squash and cucumbers to plant after the cool season vegetables are harvested. I'll buy tomato plants later if people aren't hoarding them.

I take no credit for the beautiful vegetable garden just outside our kitchen door. The previous owner, who was a Francophile, created it as a potager designed for French-style intensive gardening. The rectangular space is bound by low stucco walls topped with slate stones. Inside, there are eight 8 x 6 foot plots, four on each side of the gravel path that runs up the middle, with each plot divided in half with a long steppingstone; each plot is one step higher than the one in front. The space is so pretty that for the six years we've been here, I've enthusiastically planted it. But it seems that with each successive year, the harvests have become more meager. Raccoons ate bites out of every tomato, it seemed, the night before I intended to harvest them. Bean beetles defoliated the green beans for the last two years. Worms devoured the lovely cabbages even before they could form dense heads. Zucchini grew overnight into wooden baseball bats, then the plants wilted and died from borers. The rhubarb the previous owner had planted 10 years ago rotted during the rains of 2018 and the replacements I planted in 2019 died of drought that year in August.

I suddenly feel defeated before I even begin and I question my aspirations for this so-called Victory Garden. I remind myself that last year I had vowed to this year grow only basil, mint, cucumbers, turnips, and Swiss chard, the only vegetables that have not defeated me. Jim will just have to learn to love chard. And I had intended to plant lilies in any empty plots. Now, I look at this elegant walled garden and wonder how in the world I'll be able to actually feed us from it. I know without question that this coronavirus will get much, much worse before it gets any better. I wonder if the supermarket shelves will be empty of vegetables come summer just as the meat counter is bare now. Or if I will dare to shop. Will there be enough farmers and field hands alive to grow, harvest, and transport the produce?

Before I begin to hoe out the weeds to prepare for planting, I take a good look at my French garden – so out of place here in Appalachia. At this very moment, kale literally carpets four of the plots. In mid-October, I had sown kale seeds thickly in an attempt to make the garden look pretty when I was expecting guests, and to deter winter weeds. I'd never grown kale before. The seeds had germinated quickly and decorated the garden with foliage, but I hadn't paid much attention since then. Now, here in mid-March I had a victory harvest of perfect, unmarred, edible blue-green foliage that had survived the winter and burst forth in the coolness of March.

I studied this wonder, this mighty harvest that sprang from tiny seeds, soil and sunshine and knew I could feed us if I have to. I will adopt the spirit of a subsistence farmer and feed us from this land. I will examine every leaf of every plant and handpick the bugs, beetles, and worms. And I will share my bounty with Jeanette, my dear neighbor, as I know she will share with me."

If you want to become a vegetable gardener, you'll find many excellent online resources for growing your own small garden and composting table scraps, including "Vegetable Gardening for Beginners", (The Old Farmer's Almanac: www.almanac.com) and "How to Start Composting (yes, even in the city)", by Casey Seidenberg. (*The Washington Post:* www.washingtonpost.com, June 6, 2017)

Where the Wild Foods Are

As I have become a nibbler of violets during the current crisis, I assume other botanically minded and trained people might be eyeing the weeds in their worlds and wondering if any of them are good and safe to eat, and if it is okay to do so without harming native plant populations. While leading nature walks in the Washington, DC area during non-crisis times, I've often run into Matt Cohen along the trail, he with his group of field trip participants, I with mine. While I was teaching my group only how to identify the plants along the trail, Matt was teaching them what they could eat! Matt, a popular educator in the Washington, DC area, made sure I read the following guidelines before sharing a list of mid-Atlantic area edibles with me. Foraging is not legal in many national, state and local parks and it's up to you to find safe and lawful places to collect. Safe foraging assumes botanical knowledge of any plant you collect. **Do not collect plants to eat if you lack a botanical education. Also, unless you are a trained mycologist or are directed by one, never sample wild mushrooms.**

Because learning to forage is a lifetime undertaking, and this is not the time to flood emergency rooms with beginning foragers, it is best to learn under an expert like Matt, read edible plant books, and become part of a foraging community. Two particular field guides on my shelf jumped out at me this spring and I've been eagerly thumbing through them: *A Field Guide to Edible Wild Plants* in the Peterson Field Guide Series and Euell Gibbons's *Stalking the Wild Asparagus*.

I asked Matt what books and online resources he'd recommend to the would-be forager and he responded:

"Euell Gibbons's books are classics, but if I had to choose two guides, they'd be Peterson's field guide to edible plants (because it's easy to carry along) and then:

- *Identifying and Harvesting Edible and Medicinal Plants In Wild (and not so wild) Places*, Steve Brill — A more in depth (and fun) reference on the uses of plants (including possible medicinal uses) with detailed illustrations. This is a larger book that I use at home. Organized by season.
- I'm also a big fan of Samuel Thayer's three books: *The Forager's Harvest, Nature's Garden,* and *Incredible Wild Edibles.* They are exceptionally detailed and cover tricky look-alikes (such as common milkweed vs dogbane

and wild carrot vs poison hemlock). Each book covers 30+ plants with great photos, descriptions, and debunk some foraging myths that Gibbons's and even Brill's books have in them. They also go in depth into harvesting and preparing tricky to process foods like acorns, hickory nuts, wild rice, & cattails. The downside is there are three books and they aren't as portable as Peterson's.

- For an online resource, I like Green Deane's Eat the Weeds website."

Here are Matt's foraging guidelines, which he hands out on his walks:

- **Only eat something if you are absolutely sure of its identification.** There are a minority of plants and mushrooms that can kill even if you eat a small amount. There are many more that can cause gastrointestinal distress and other discomfort.
- When sampling something for the first time, especially if you have food sensitivities, try a small amount and wait an hour or two. If it sits well with you, try a larger portion and wait again. Everyone has different body chemistries and may react to new food unpredictably.
- All edible wild mushrooms should be cooked, unless you are told otherwise, before being consumed. (See note above about mushrooms.)
- Cultivate a respectful attitude when foraging. Think of yourself as a gardener and nature is our shared yard. When harvesting plants, only take from species where there is an abundant population. Rare and threatened native plants should be avoided altogether. Invasive, exotic plants can be harvested to your heart's content and beyond! Consider giving something back to nature when you take — pick up trash, pull invasive plants, plant natives in your yard, etc.

- Don't collect plants in areas that may be polluted: roadsides, railroad corridors, places where pesticides have been applied, bodies of polluted water, etc. Plants and mushrooms can not only have contamination on the outside, but they can also uptake poisons in the ground or water. This especially applies if you plan to eat large portions of what you are collecting.
- Learn to identify poison ivy and other plants that can cause skin irritations. Check for ticks after a walk — they can transmit Lyme disease and other illnesses.
- If you are sensitive to stinging insects, be sure to bring along medication (it's rare to get stung on my walks, but it does occasionally happen)."

Unless you have botanical knowledge, or are collecting under the direction of someone who does, it's safest to leave the wild foods in the wild for the birds and other creatures whose livelihoods depend upon them.

After I carefully reviewed Matt's foraging guidelines, he was then willing to share a list of edible plants growing wild in our region. He describes these plants as "mostly non-natives or weedy natives." He notes that in the Washington area (early spring): "There's lots out there right now. I've been collecting common violet leaves and flowers, dandelion flowers and leaves, common chickweed, hairy bittercress, wood sorrels, lamb's quarters, redbud flowers and field garlic right from my backyard to make some fresh, healthy salads. All of these can be cooked in soups or stir fried."

Matt has included culinary suggestions for many species of edible plant with his list. The notes within square parentheses are mine.

"*Garlic mustard (Alliaria petiolata)* — Any part: roots, leaves, flower buds, flowers, stem and even seeds. Garlic mustard pesto/spread from leaves. Add to salads, soups, fried greens. Root for horseradish substitute. [You'll be doing native plant populations a favor if you harvest this invasive plant in North America!]

Stinging Nettle (Urtica dioica) — Top 4" or so of plant in the spring, use gloves. Boiled greens — upon a few seconds of contact with boiling water the sting goes away. I like to add to soups.

Japanese knotweed (Reynoutria japonica; Polygonum cuspidatum) — Shoots — raw, pickles, jellies and compote. [Very invasive in eastern North America and elsewhere.]

Bamboo (Phyllostachys spp.) — Shoots — generally should be boiled in water for at least 30 minutes water is then drained off. They can be eaten as is, soups, fried, pickled, etc.

Greenbrier (Smilax rotundifolia) — Any soft, newly growing leaves, shoots, tendril can be eaten raw. Can cook anyway you'd like but I prefer raw.

Lady's thumb (Persicaria maculosa; Polygonum persicaria) — Young sprouts and tender tips for salads, cooked greens.

Purslane (Portulaca oleracea) — Stems & leaves, salads, pickled, add to tabbouleh. [Henry David Thoreau wrote in *Walden,* "I have made a satisfactory dinner, satisfactory on several accounts, simply off a dish of purslane *(Portulaca oleracea)* which I gathered in my cornfield, boiled and salted."]

Pokeweed (Phytolacca americana) — Shoots - only gather shoots less than 2' tall, great vegetable, need to cook in at least 2 changes of boiling water. Discard water after each boiling. **[Beware though, as the mature plant and its berries are poisonous to humans.]**

Black locust (Robinia pseudoacacia) — Flowers —raw, at peak they taste like peas with a bit of sweetness. Tree is invasive in Europe.

Serviceberry (Shadbush or *Juneberry) (Amelanchier* spp.) — Fruits, common landscape plant.

Mulberry (Morus spp.) — Ripe fruits, raw, jams, fruit leather, baked desserts.

Sumac (Rhus spp.) — Tender new growth, berry clusters — sour seasoning, wild lemonade. (Any of the *Rhus* species with red berries: staghorn, smooth, winged are what you want to look for. To see if the berries are good to use for sumac lemonade, touch them with your finger and taste where you touched it. If it's sour, it's ready to use. **Of course, avoid poison sumac which has white berry clusters and tends to grow in wet, swampy areas.)**

Daylily (Hemerocallis fulva) — roots, shoots, flower buds, flowers. flower buds are my favorite, but eat in moderation as many people get diarrhea from eating too much.

Cattail (Typha latifolia) — Shoots, unopened male flowers, pollen, roots for starch [Euell Gibbons calls cattails the "supermarket of the swamps."]

Wineberry (Rubus phoenicolasius) , and other brambles *(Rubus* spp.) — Fruits straight, jams, desserts. [Very invasive in mid-Atlantic area of the US.]

Chinese Chestnuts (Castanea mollisima), Black Walnuts (Juglans nigra) — late summer.

Wild mints (Mentha spp.*)* — Flavoring, teas.

Pawpaws (Asimina triloba), Persimmons (Diospyros virginiana)

Shiso (Beefsteak plant, Perilla) (Perilla frutescens) — Leaves used for flavoring in Japanese and Korean cuisine.

Acorns (from Quercus spp.*)* — From any oak tree, largest & mildest tasting generally are the best to start with. Need to leech off tannins by soaking in water repeatedly. Sawtooth oak acorns work well. Acorns have been a staple source of calories for many cultures. Koreans still use them today.

Maple (Acer) sap — Drink straight, base for tea, boil down to make syrup or sugar."

In order to avoid trips to the grocery store and to make up for the fact that we're all out of hard-to-come-by vitamin C tablets, I've been sampling some of the wild plants on this list on my walks in the neighborhood and on a farm I visit near Sugarloaf Mountain: my morning violets and redbud flowers; wild garlic; chickweed; and dandelion. I'm planning to make teas with young white pine needles and spicebush twigs. However, unless you have botanical knowledge, or are collecting under the direction of someone who does, it's safest to leave the wild foods in the wild for the birds and other creatures whose livelihoods depend upon them.

The Garden as Refuge

Although I've focused here on gardening and foraging for food during our current crisis, I don't want to overlook the importance of the garden as a refuge, a place of beauty and serenity, representing hard work, but offering the gardener and the garden visitor a place of peace and rejuvenation.

Soon after the corona crisis became real here in Maryland, I stumbled upon two Audubon Naturalist Society volunteers with their trowels, who were digging weeds—six feet apart—in the Blair Native Plant Garden at the Woodend sanctuary (ANS headquarters). Gayle Countryman-Mills, who was sitting on a log in the garden, and Sarah Richards, who was kneeling, were clearly enjoying the spring sun and the earthy smells emanating from the garden soil. Gayle told me that working in the garden was "very Zen" and that watching the plants grow and blossom and produce fruit through the seasons was a constant source of inspiration. Sarah said that each of them has a garden at home but there was special joy in working in a garden that could enlighten and delight many visitors. As I watched them dig their trowels in the dirt, their faces lit by the early spring sun, I could tell there was no place on earth that they would rather be.

Chapter Six

Transformation: Insights and Commitment During a Time of Crisis

Woodland Walk (Photo by Ana Ka'ahanui)

And once the storm is over, you won't remember how you made it through, how you managed to survive. You won't even be sure whether the storm is really over. But one thing is certain. When you come out of the storm, you won't be the same person who walked in. That's what this storm is all about.

Haruki Murakami

As a species we have tremendous faith in our ability to transform our surroundings and prevail in any crisis through human will and know-how, backed up when deemed necessary by human might. And yet now, a tiny microbe has brought the whole human world to its knees. At this writing, children in many parts of the world are out of school and half the earth's human population is under shelter in place orders or recommendations. Many people are losing their jobs and the world's economy is teetering on the brink of recession or something worse.

For those of us who observe nature closely on a regular basis, this virus may seem less alien. During recent years I've watched two native tree species decimated by invasive insect pests, and a fungus that felled 4 billion chestnut trees in the eastern US during the twentieth century is still actively killing trees. I already knew from the plant world that global travel has unwelcome consequences. And, climate change favors pathogens of many kinds. In the American West the too-warm winters have failed to kill beetle species, which have wreaked havoc on conifer trees in many states.

The world-renowned conservation biologist Thomas Lovejoy writes: "Some people are viewing the pandemic as nature fighting back against all that has been and continues to be done to it. It is human behavior and disrespect for nature that have been the cause. Further, as we cope with the pandemic, climate change is marching ahead causing strong ripples of change in all ecosystems easily tipping the balance in favor of pathogens currently unknown to us.

The wise way forward is to invest in conservation and science, and to embrace nature and the glorious variety of life with which we share this planet. A healthy future for humanity and a healthy biodiverse planet go hand in hand."[9]

I wondered if in some way the current crisis could help bring us closer to nature and deepen our understanding of how we're interconnected. We are in the position of both responding to a natural crisis, and seeking nature as a balm for our fears and anxieties. Could this tie us deeper to the natural web and help us to gain new insights and resilience? Here's what I heard from some of my friends and colleagues, many of whom remarked on the unexpected gift of *time*:

"I now have time to observe and reflect on these issues..." Betsy Bass

My friend Betsy Bass, who lives on the side of Sugarloaf Mountain in Maine, a more famous and lofty peak than Maryland's Sugarloaf, observes: "The world is one large web. Actions in one part of the world impact eventually all parts of the world. We have seen this with the coronavirus. But polluting our waters, cutting forests, building too densely, and removing wetlands all negatively impact our wildlife, migrating birds, the air we breathe, and contribute to climate change. I now have time to observe and reflect on these issues and consider how I can continue to help keep our world – people, nature, wildlife, and climate – healthy."

"I know I am taking the time to listen..." Sandy Willen

My friend Sandy Willen, who walks daily in Washington, DC observes: "What is different is the amount of time I have to observe up close and personally the blooming flowers, the greening of the trees, the daily subtle changes, the sounds and the fragrances of spring and, most delightful, the songs of the birds. Is it my imagination or are the birds singing louder than ever this year? I know I am taking the time to listen and, for once, nature and these birds have my undivided attention."

"Now that the world has stopped, I have time to get into a daily walking rhythm..." Clay Jenkinson

Historian, lecturer, actor and author Clay Jenkinson's professional life involves constant travel around the country and the world. Now that he's grounded at his home in Bismarck, North Dakota, he reports: "I'm walking five miles a day now, every day. Since I live on the Great Plains and it is springtime, my quest is to hear my first meadowlark of the year. The western meadowlark has the most beautiful bird song I have ever heard...

My normal life does not allow much time for walking outside. I work out in airport hotels, do plenty of walking getting from Terminal A to Terminal B, but most of my movement is thanks to internal combustion engines. Now that the world has stopped, I have time to get into a daily walking rhythm…I invariably cheer up when I take long walks, get back into my body, gain solace from fresh air, and gain confidence from my capacity to propel myself through the world on my legs. Whenever I feel overwrought by the pandemic, I get out on the walking paths on the north end of my town…I have not been able to go on long hikes yet, because I am trying not to use my car unless necessary, but when the weather warms up a bit, I will get myself to the badlands and butte country of western North Dakota for some serious hiking."

This is the refrain that I'm hearing again and again during this crisis, especially from nature lovers: "I now have time." And much of this time, in the absence of the usual daily routines and distractions, is spent walking, quietly observing, and reflecting. And reflections often turn to gratitude for the continuity of the natural world. People are noting that they are seeing more closely and feeling more deeply.

Artist and environmental activist Ginny Barnes of Montgomery County, Maryland notes: "My walks are now solitary. I feel a stillness inside that comes from slowing down. Though I miss tree and wildflower-loving friends, the connection to the natural world is deepening and filling me with hope and newfound joy. Just a simple thing like weeding in the garden has become meditation."

Author and communications expert Tim Ward wrote from the Eastern Shore of Maryland: "I walk along a mostly deserted beach two or three times each day (normally it gets busy in spring – not this year)…When I get stressed and anxious, I look at the seabirds and dolphins. They are unconcerned. I realize the Earth carries on, barely noticing our self-inflicted wound. I find this reminder of humanity's insignificance strangely comforting."

Environmental writer and retired National Oceanic & Atmospheric Administration (NOAA) analyst Ellen Gordon observes: "Sometimes as I walk back to the house from the barn, I stop for a moment to drink in the sight of the horses, the woods, and the nearby mountain—always there. If it's morning, the songbirds will be singing joyfully from the woods, and the squirrels will invariably be chasing after each other up and down the old trees. If it's evening, the spring peepers will be madly chorusing, the wood frogs will be quacking and the peacocks from the farm over the hill will be mewling. And if night's falling, the coyotes will be yipping and howling. As always."

Pomona College Professor Char Miller writes from his home in Claremont, California:

"Look up. Here as elsewhere, that possibility has been clouded by the emissions we pump into the air. Now, with so many of us working from home, so many cars parked, trains, planes and trucks idled, the sky has dazzled. Day and night. My evening stroll is complicated by trying to put one foot in front of the other while craning my neck to pan the star-lit world above. Then, somewhere to my west, perhaps high in the sentinel-like stone pine at the end of the block, a Great Horned Owl calls. Grounded."

I find great comfort in these personal stories of resilient appreciation while I struggle to come to terms with the pandemic and the personal misery it brings. Clearly we can hold hope and resolve in our hearts alongside our uncertainty, fear and empathy for those who are suffering.

Today there is a global glimmer of something resembling hope in the crisis for the world at large. Reports are trickling in from around the world of clearer skies and cleaner air, of sea turtles nesting unimpeded on deserted beaches, whales birthing calves in waters free of cruise ships and tour boats, and even seismologists able to read earthquakes more readily due to the lessening of human-generated noise.

On a more mundane level, with all of our usual stuff so hard to get, will we become more apt to reuse and recycle? I know I am already replacing paper with cloth whenever I can. As in any crisis, we must learn to live with uncertainty, and especially during this pandemic, humility. May this global episode help us to discover new and more sustaining ways of interacting with the natural world. We are part of nature and we share in nature's resilience.

"When you come out of the storm, you won't be the same person who walked in."

Chapter Seven

Notes from the Field: Stories of Resilience

Snow falling on balsam firs (Photo by Betsy Bass)

I am blessed with family, friends and colleagues all over the US who are deeply connected with nature. Near the beginning of the current crisis, I wrote to some of them, and asked them how they were sustaining their connection with nature, and what nature was teaching them. I want to share with you their observations and wisdom."With so much time suddenly on my hands, I've been exploring nature without a 'to do' list. Patches of woods or parks that I previously whizzed by on my bike — 'too barren' or 'too disturbed' I now stop to investigate. This strange time has given me an open and expansive feeling that I remember from summers growing up in Florida. If I feel like it, I will sit and watch a single robin for an hour. I have nothing more pressing to do, so why not?"

Sadie Dingfelder, Washington, DC.

"I walk or amble slowly now, seeking smaller and smaller evanescent beauty. In my watching, I have moved from the big things — Yoshino cherry trees, magnolias with magenta-painted china cups for blossoms, soaring and nesting Bald Eagles, diving winter ducks, pounding Pileated woodpeckers — to looking, on my knees, at the tiny pink stripes of spring beauties, as they seek light and life amidst the leaf litter, the comic pantaloons of Dutchman's breeches, the small, ragged, yellow daisy tops of golden ragwort, bursting forth from the tight, purplish black BBs that are their buds."
Robert K. Musil, Bethesda, Maryland

"My heart always swells as I see the US Capitol. It is one of incalculable joys of living in the nation's capital. I reside in a city of monuments. I need only walk three miles from my home to gaze on democratic institutions. I feel immensely grateful that our forefathers had the vision to create the National Mall so that we "the people" could look down a stretch of verdant lawn "America's front yard" to see the Washington Monument while standing on the West Lawn of the US Capitol. It is even more important to me during the pandemic to get out and commune with nature. I know my stress is reduced from the minute that I start walking among the trees."
Terri Markle, Washington, DC

"I am bicycling 14 miles each morning in a loop, up the C&O Canal towpath to the Marsden Bridge, then back down the bike lane of MacArthur Boulevard. This morning I heard my first warbler of spring—Louisiana Waterthrush. I also stopped to commune with an adult male Pileated Woodpecker, talking quietly to him as he foraged about 15 feet from me at eye level.
I am grateful for nature and the pleasing solitude of my bike

ride along the great Potomac River. I am spending more energy looking around me and seeking the wild and natural." Bruce M. Beehler, Bethesda, Maryland

"Narrowing my range has widened my perceptions; I have to listen more carefully, look more closely, smell more discriminatingly (or, to be honest, think about what I am inhaling). On rainy mornings—and we have actually had some this March in LA County—I have mapped my path so that I pass close to the California Botanical Garden and its heaven-scent coastal sage biota; the air is perfumed. I then veer toward the nearest flood channel to listen to water rippling, sluicing over wet concrete."
Char Miller, Claremont, California

"This wooded landscape is poised on the brink of spring — the wood frogs are singing in the wetlands and the dawn chorus of birdsong has begun. There is still sap dripping from the maple trees and the final bits of snow are hanging on in the deep crevasses of the glacial rock piles. These are the things that, in another time, might have slipped my attention. On a long walk in Great Mountain Forest the other day, I was treated to the sight of a bald eagle making a successful catch in Chrissy Pond. I am making time for nature and trying to breathe into my worries and cares. I think it is helping."
Betsy Childs Gill, Norfolk, Connecticut

"I am making a ritual of going out each morning—even if only for a very short time, to meet/greet the new day and listen to the birdsong. Watching the morning sunrise can give you a new sense of hope for the day ahead.

Combining the early morning scents and sounds with the prospect of another whole day is so restorative and inspirational....

I'm also making somewhat of a ritual of going out at the end of the day/early evening.

There is a special almost sacred beauty that comes every evening from twilight to the hour beyond.

Watch the sky as it fades into darkness, again listen to the birds as they settle down for the night."

Carole Bergmann, Clarksburg, Maryland

"I am sensing Mother Earth is able to breathe more fully. I read that the skies in China are clear with fewer fossil fuels polluting them. As I am learning about the connection between the spread of the virus and climate change, it's made me even more committed to doing something about our climate crisis."

Emily Ecker, Bryant Pond, Maine

"Every afternoon my four boys and I head to our 'secret spot' in the neighborhood woods where we play, play, play, gloriously unplugged and away from reality and people, escaping our new normal of too many screens during online work and school. Yesterday, as we approached our spot in the woods where we've never seen another person, we heard music. It was totally magical, a flautist was practicing in our spot and happily provided the most gorgeous background music to our afternoon nature play.

There is so much suffering in the world right now but there is also beauty. It's refreshing to be reminded there are always silver linings if you look at something just right."

Stephanie Bozzo, Rockville, Maryland

"While we humans are hunkered down across the globe, Mother Earth is healing. For me, it's a hopeful counterpoint to the pandemic."

Lindsay Beane, Baltimore, Maryland

"I have always used my time in Rock Creek Park to meditate through birding and running while also ruminating on any questions or issues I need to work through. Now I am using my woodsy time to simply escape, not dwell on, the constant noise – the noise of bad news, of fear, of the unknown, of worries – and replace it with nature's noise: peeping spring peepers, singing songbirds, babbling waters, rustling leaves, howling coyotes and screaming foxes. It works for as long as I am in there! I am learning to embrace what will be just as the birds embrace their natural instincts to move north, mate and nurture future generations year after year."
Betsy Lovejoy, Washington, DC

"Idaho state went on 'lock-down' a few days ago, although many of us had been self-isolating to one degree or another for several weeks. During this time of being 'shut in', my daily walks out in my beautiful neighborhood, on the beach of the lake, and on my local hiking hill (Tubbs Hill), are essential to my sense of mental well-being, need for exercise and fresh air, and a sense that nature is still intact in many ways and is there to nurture us, heal us, and give us hope for the future."
Pam Davies, Coeur d'Alene, Idaho

"I'll be getting myself to the badlands of North Dakota and the Little Missouri River valley in the next couple of weeks to see the prairie pasqueflowers in bloom. We call them crocuses. They are, in my view, the most beautiful of wildflowers."
Clay Jenkinson, Bismarck, North Dakota

"Nature is saving me. I have severe PTSD and nature offers me a quiet place where I'm completely okay and safe. When I go on trails with more people on them, I start getting really spooked. So I've been scouting out trails that are very quiet."
Clare Kelley, Tucson, Arizona

"My mother had two expressions that ring truer now than ever... 'If you've got your health, you've got everything,' and 'Even when it rains, I believe in the sun!' Never has her wisdom been more relevant...COVID-19 has changed so much of my daily life activities that time spent in nature, which I have always enjoyed, has become even more important. Feeling the sunshine, taking an extra-long breath, and expressing my gratitude for my good health are now my most cherished daily activities."
Sandy Willen, Washington, DC

"My ongoing activities – Maine Lakes Society Board, Project Feederwatch, enjoying and appreciating the natural environment through walks, sports, and photography, continue. But we all have more time to be outside, notice what is happening, become more involved in protecting our natural areas, and mitigate our impact on speeding up climate change. Today, more than ever before, we should protect the National Parks and other public lands, endangered species, water quality and many other aspects of our natural world."
Betsy Bass, Carrabassett Valley, Maine

"The crisis itself feels all the more frightening as a harbinger of the risks to the natural world as a whole. Admonitions about social distancing to avert infection — 'we need to act now and act quickly to prevent the worst from happening' — are readily applicable to climate change. So I get out when I can to enjoy the truly great outdoors — but worry, is this all a warning — even a perverse practice drill — for something even more dangerous and unfathomable?"
Ralph Buglass, Rockville, Maryland

"I went straight to the compost pile weeks ago as the pandemic became real.

This diversion connects me to the earth in a fundamental way I can't explain. I love digging around, sifting organic soil from woody debris that didn't decompose overwinter. These twigs and branches have to make their way into a new compost pile. So I take aim and send the branch flying, smiling with each toss.By the time I have dug deep into this year's rich organic muck, I have forgotten the news of the day and my to-do list."
Tina Thieme Brown, Barnesville, Maryland

"The pace of life has slowed—human, day to day life, that is. Some things are exactly as they always are; the horses still need to be fed twice/day. They've begun the annual shedding of their winter coats; to help with their itchiness, I like to spend extra time brushing them even when I'm not prepping them for a ride. It's a kind of anchoring, that their needs haven't changed a bit just because there's a frightening pandemic sweeping our world.

The chickens are pleased with the early spring, charging around their yard scratching up worms and pecking up delicious bites of the juicy, aptly named 'chickweed.' They're utterly unaware of how surreal the passing days feel to their people, and because the increasing light encourages them to lay, they are happily providing an abundance of eggs—just as they do every year at this time."
Ellen Gordon, Comus, Maryland

"When we moved, at the top of my wish list was trail access within walking distance of our new home. Never have I been more grateful for that wish coming true! I have been getting out every evening by myself for what I call my 'cocktail walkabout,' while Sam puts the girls to bed. The neighborhood is so peaceful and beautiful then, I love seeing all the homes lit up and neighbors cozy in their kitchens."
Lacey Brown, Silver Spring, Maryland

"Everything seems new in light of this crisis. Compelled to be home, I really look at what is growing, living, emerging. I study what I see more closely. Then come inside to field guides and books on natural history. I sit outside watching birds at the feeder, wildflowers and trees emerging into blessed spring. I feel more spiritually close to nature than ever before."
Ginny Barnes, Potomac, Maryland

"I sense a greater stillness...I am aware that many others outside are appreciating the treasures of spring more and aren't just blowing by them. I think we all are appreciating the resilience of nature."
Marney Bruce, Bethesda, Maryland

"During this time of uncertainty there is solace in the predictable unpredictable variability of the coming of spring. The bluebirds are stopping by the bird houses, the sparrows are joining the goldfinches and juncos at the feeder. Tiny buds, loud overflowing streams, deer in the lower field and the early grass poking up in the lawn (sure to draw the waking bear)."
Dr. Catherine Cornell, Plymouth, New Hampshire

"It's hard to marginalize other people when we are in this coronavirus pandemic together. Other than the practical paranoia of standing too close to someone in the checkout line, I see people extending kindness toward each other. Especially in the neighborhood and in the local park. No matter what we look like or whatever subgroup we are supposed to be part of, we share a smile and a knowing nod of recognition under the sun and the trees."
Stella Tarnay, Washington, DC

Acknowledgments

My heartfelt thanks to Nature Educator Wendy Paulson for your eloquent foreword for the book and for all you have taught me about birding and ecology. I thank my family, friends and colleagues throughout the US who responded so thoughtfully to my questions about how you are connecting with nature during the current crisis: Ellie Anderson, Ginny Barnes, Betsy Bass, Lindsay Beane, Bruce Beehler, Carole Bergmann, Tina Thieme Brown, Marney Bruce, Ralph Bugloss, Dr. Catherine Cornell, Pam Davies, Sadie Dingfelder, Emily Ecker, Betsy Childs Gill, Ellen Gordon, Ellen Gordon Gordon, Clay Jenkinson, Ana Ka'ahanui, Clare Kelley, Betsy Lovejoy, Terri Markle, Char Miller, Robert Musil, Anne Sturm, Stella Tarnay, and Sandy Willen. I thank Park Rx America Founder, Dr. Robert Zarr, Science and Nature Writer, Gabriel Popkin, and Artist and Birder Polly Alexander for sharing your knowledge and perspectives with me. Thank you to Conservation Biologist Thomas Lovejoy for sharing your wonderful essay, *Pandemic Perspectives*, with me. I'm very grateful to Lisa Alexander, Executive Director of the Audubon Naturalist Society (ANS), Stephanie Bozzo, ANS Nature Preschool Director, and Stephanie Mason, ANS Senior Naturalist, for sharing your wisdom, knowledge and expertise with me and with the Washington, DC nature community during this difficult time. Thanks, too, to ANS volunteers Gayle Countryman-Mills and Sarah Richards, with whom I enjoyed a delightful impromptu meeting in the Blair Native Plant Garden. Thank you Arborist and Nature Educator Lacey Brown for taking time away from your many creative home-schooling projects to share your thoughts and ideas for this book. Heartfelt thanks to Photographer and Author Susan Austin Roth, for reporting on your "Victory Garden," and for contributing photography for this book. Thank you to Matt Cohen of Matt's Habitats for your expert foraging advice (and cautions). Thank you to Ana Ka'ahanui and Stella Tarnay, Co-Founders of Capital Nature, for sharing your knowledge of Citizen Science. And thank you, Ana, for your nature photographs. I'm grateful to Kate Maynor for your words of encouragement about nature journaling and I thank Tina Thieme Brown for describing your art process in the field. As always, my agent, Marilyn Allen, has been by my side with good advice and inspiration. Ari Fisher, "The Tech Mensch," has rescued me many times! John Hunt of John Hunt Publishing and Tim Ward, publisher of Changemakers Books, had the ground-breaking idea to publish this series of "Resilience" books within a tight window to help people through the crisis and I thank you, and my fellow "Resilience" authors for your vision and speed! The brilliant editing team with whom I worked on my forthcoming (yet previously written) book, *Finding Solace at Theodore Roosevelt Island,* reassembled for this project: Publisher Tim Ward and fellow Author Michelle Auerbach. Thank you both! Many thanks to copy editor, Krystina Kellingley. I also thank my children, Sophie and Jesse Choukas-Bradley, for your astute editing of this book, and all of my books. As always, I thank my husband, Jim Choukas-Bradley, and our children and extended family for sharing your contagious delight in the natural world.

Endnotes

1. Yoshifumi Miyazaki, *Shinrin-Yoku: The Japanese Art of Forest Bathing* (Portland, OR: Timber Press, 2018), 110.
2. John Muir, My First Summer in the Sierra (St. Louis, MO: J Missouri, 2018, originally published 1911. Passage written on July 31, 1869), 106.
3. John Muir, "Mormon Lilies," San Francisco Daily Evening Bulletin, July 19, 1877, reprinted in Steep Trails (Boston and New York: Houghton Mifflin Company, 1918), chapter 9.
4. John Muir, John of the Mountains: The Unpublished Journals of John Muir, edited by Linnie Marsh Wolfe (Madison, WI: University of Wisconsin Press, 1938, republished 1979), 439.
5. Theodore Roosevelt, *An Autobiography* (New York, NY: Charles Scribner's Sons, 1926, originally published, 1913), 318.
6. Theodore Roosevelt, *Outdoor Pastimes of an American Hunter* (Mechanicsburg, PA: Stackpole Books, The Classics of American Sport Series, 1990, originally 1905), 339.
7. Theodore Roosevelt, *An Autobiography*, 318-9.
8. Ibid., 319.
9. Thomas Lovejoy, *Pandemic Perspectives* (essay shared in an email, April 5, 2020)

About the Author

Melanie Choukas-Bradley is the award-winning author of several nature books, including *Finding Solace at Theodore Roosevelt Island, A Year in Rock Creek Park, City of Trees* and *The Joy of Forest Bathing*. Melanie brought her love of trees and nature to Washington, DC, following a childhood spent wandering the woods and fields of southern Vermont. She leads nature hikes, tree tours, forest-bathing walks, and kayak trips for many non-profit organizations in the Washington area and in the American West and New England.

Books by Melanie Choukas-Bradley

Finding Solace at Theodore Roosevelt Island (2020).
Illustrated by Tina Thieme Brown.
The Joy of Forest Bathing: —Reconnect with Wild Places and Rejuvenate Your Life (2018). Illustrated by Lieke van der Vorst.
A Year in Rock Creek Park: The Wild, Wooded Heart of Washington, DC (2014). Photography by Susan Austin Roth.
City of Trees: —The Complete Field Guide to the Trees of Washington, DC (2008; 1987; originally published as *City of Trees: —The Complete Botanical and Historical Guide to the Trees of Washington, DC*, 1981). Illustrated and co-authored by Polly Alexander.
An Illustrated Guide to Eastern Woodland Wildflowers and Trees: —350 Plants Observed at Sugarloaf Mountain, Maryland (2007; 2004). Illustrated and co-authored by Tina Thieme Brown.
Sugarloaf: —The Mountain's History, Geology and Natural Lore (2003). Illustrated and co-authored by Tina Thieme Brown.

TRANSFORMATION

The *Resilience* Series

The Resilience Series is a collaborative effort by the authors of Changemakers Books in response to the 2020 coronavirus epidemic. Each concise volume offers expert advice and practical exercises for mastering specific skills and abilities. Our intention is that by strengthening your resilience, you can better survive and even thrive in a time of crisis.

Resilience: Adapt and Plan for the New Abnormal of the COVID-19 Coronavirus Pandemic
by Gleb Tsipursky

COVID-19 has demonstrated clearly that businesses, nonprofits, individuals, and governments are terrible at dealing effectively with large-scale disasters that take the form of slow-moving train-wrecks. Using cutting-edge research in cognitive neuroscience and behavioral economics on dangerous judgment errors (cognitive biases), this book first explains why we respond so poorly to slow-moving, high-impact, and long-term crises. Next, the book shares research-based strategies for how organizations and individuals can adapt effectively to the new abnormal of the COVID-19 pandemic and similar disasters. Finally, it shows how to develop an effective strategic plan and make the best major decisions in the context of the uncertainty and ambiguity brought about by COVID-19 and other slow-moving large-scale catastrophes. The author, a cognitive neuroscientist and behavioral economist and CEO of the consulting, coaching, and training firm Disaster Avoidance Experts, combines research-based strategies with real-life stories from his business and nonprofit clients as they adapt to the pandemic.

Resilience: Aging with Vision, Hope and Courage in a Time of Crisis
by John C. Robinson

This book is for those over 65 wrestling with fear, despair, insecurity, and loneliness in these frightening times. A blend of psychology, self-help, and spirituality, it's meant for all who hunger for facts, respect, compassion, and meaningful resources to light their path ahead. The 74-year-old author's goal is to move readers from fear and paralysis to growth and engagement: "Acknowledging the inspiring resilience and wisdom of our hard-won maturity, I invite you on a personal journey of transformation and renewal into a new consciousness and a new world."

Resilience: Connecting with Nature in a Time of Crisis
by Melanie Choukas-Bradley

Nature is one of the best medicines for difficult times. An intimate awareness of the natural world, even within the city, can calm anxieties and help create healthy perspectives. This book will inspire and guide you as you deal with the current crisis, or any personal or worldly distress. The author is a naturalist and certified forest therapy guide who leads nature and forest bathing walks for many organizations in Washington, DC and the American West. Learn from her the Japanese art of "forest bathing": how to tune in to the beauty and wonder around you with all your senses, even if your current sphere is a tree outside the window or a wild backyard. Discover how you can become a backyard naturalist, learning about the trees, wildflowers, birds and animals near your home. Nature immersion during stressful times can bring comfort and joy as well as opportunities for personal growth, expanded vision and transformation.

Resilience: Going Within in a Time of Crisis
by P.T. Mistlberger

During a time of crisis, we are presented with something of a fork in the road; we either look within and examine ourselves, or engage in distractions and go back to sleep. This book is intended to be a companion for men and women dedicated to their inner journey. Written by the author of seven books and founder of several personal growth communities and esoteric schools, each chapter offers different paths for exploring your spiritual frontier: advanced meditation techniques, shadow work, conscious relating, dream work, solo retreats, and more. In traversing these challenging times, let this book be your guide.

Resilience: Grow Stronger in a Time of Crisis
by Linda Ferguson

Many of us have wondered how we would respond in the midst of a crisis. You hope that difficult times could bring out the best in you. Some become stronger, more resilient and more innovative under pressure. You hope that you will too. But you are afraid that crisis may bring out your anxiety, your fears and your weakest communication. No one knows when the crisis will pass and things will get better. That's out of your hands. But *you* can get better. All it takes is an understanding of how human beings function at their best, the willpower to make small changes in perception and behavior, and a vision of a future that is better than today. In the pages of this book, you will learn to create the conditions that allow your best self to show up and make a difference – for you and for others.

Resilience: Handling Anxiety in a Time of Crisis
by George Hofmann

It's a challenging time for people who experience anxiety, and even people who usually don't experience it are finding their moods are getting the better of them. Anxiety hits hard and its symptoms are unmistakable, but sometimes in the rush and confusion of uncertainty we miss those symptoms until it's too late. When things seem to be coming undone, it's still possible to recognize the onset of anxiety and act to prevent the worst of it. The simple steps taught in this book can help you overcome the turmoil.

Resilience: The Life-Saving Skill of Story
by Michelle Auerbach

Storytelling covers every skill we need in a crisis. We need to share information about how to be safe, about how to live together, about what to do and not do. We need to talk about what is going on in ways that keep us from freaking out. We need to change our behavior as a human race to save each other and ourselves. We need to imagine a possible future different from the present and work on how to get there. And we need to do it all without falling apart. This book will help people in any field and any walk of life to become better storytellers and immediately unleash the power to teach, learn, change, soothe, and create community to activate ourselves and the people around us.

Resilience: Navigating Loss in a Time of Crisis
by Jules De Vitto

This book explores the many forms of loss that can happen in times of crisis. These losses can range from loss of business, financial security, routine, structure to the deeper losses of meaning, purpose or identity. The author draws on her background in transpersonal psychology, integrating spiritual insights and mindfulness practices to take the reader on a journey in which to help them navigate the stages of uncertainty that follow loss. The book provides several practical activities, guided visualization and meditations to cultivate greater resilience, courage and strength and also explores the potential to find greater meaning and purpose through times of crisis.

Resilience: Virtually Speaking
Communicating at a Distance
by Teresa Erickson and Tim Ward

To adapt to a world where you can't meet face-to-face – with air travel and conferences cancelled, teams working from home – leaders, experts, managers and professionals all need to master the skills of virtual communication. Written by the authors of *The Master Communicator's Handbook*, this book tells you how to create impact with your on-screen presence, use powerful language to motivate listening, and design compelling visuals. You will also learn techniques to prevent your audience from losing attention, to keep them engaged from start to finish, and to create a lasting impact.

Resilience: Virtual Teams
Holding the Center When You Can't Meet Face-to-Face
by Carlos Valdes-Dapena

In the face of the COVID-19 virus organizations large and small are shuttering offices and factories, requiring as much work as possible be done from people's homes. The book draws on the insights of the author's earlier book, *Lessons from Mars,* providing a set of the powerful tools and exercises developed within the

Mars Corporation to create high performance teams. These tools have been adapted for teams suddenly forced to work apart, in many cases for the first time. These simple secrets and tested techniques have been used by thousands of teams who know that creating a foundation of team identity and shared meaning makes them resilient, even in a time of crisis.